Liberal democracie
challenge since the ~~*j*~~
Edgar's discussion
national populism –
both clear and concise analysis with a compelling case for action.

> – **Jonathan Portes**, Professor of Economics and Public Policy at King's College London, author and *Byline Times* contributor.

This brilliant book tells us concisely and sharply why we should fear the rise of national populists and what we do to halt the politics they peddle.

> – **Neal Lawson**, Director of Compass

There is no longer a guard rail between democratic politics and populism. A nationalist poison has entered the bloodstream of parliaments across the West. But it's no time for panic and despair. Here's a vital book from seasoned political writers to show how to push it back into the dark zone it came from, with a hope for democratic renewal. Read it to revive optimism that it can and must be overcome.

> – **Polly Toynbee**, *Guardian* columnist

Everyone needs a little black book! This is a brilliant analysis of the most serious challenge to liberal democracy – the global rise of right-wing populism. Two great political commentators examine its root causes and its well travelled trajectories at home and abroad: attacks on the rule of law, a contempt for international institutions, the sowing of social divisions and the scapegoating of the 'other'. How can we stem the tide? This is vital reading.

> – **Helena Kennedy** KC

First Edition

THE LITTLE BLACK BOOK OF THE POPULIST RIGHT

—

By

Jon Bloomfield and David Edgar

Executive Series Editor

Kyle Taylor

LONDON, UNITED KINGDOM

Byline Books

London, United Kingdom

First published in the United Kingdom of Great Britain
and Northern Ireland by Byline Books, 2024

Text copyright © Jon Bloomfield and David Edgar, 2024

Cover design by Steve Leard

Copy editing/layout by Prepare to Publish

Printed in Great Britain by Clays Ltd

ISBN UK: 978-1-916754-06-5

CONTENTS

___

FOREWORD

——

Byline Books published the first 'Little Black Book', on *Data and Democracy*, in March 2021. I believed that the concept of short, accessible but deeply researched books aimed at explaining complex topics using everyday language could not only find an audience, but develop into a series that continuously tackles the biggest issues of the day. Part of that vision included expanding the series to give voice to other authors expert in a growing range of issues. While I had the privilege of authoring the first four titles in the series and we have now sold over 10,000 copies, it is with immense pride that **Byline Books** brings you our first title by other authors.

The Little Black Book of the Populist Right has been expertly crafted by Jon Bloomfield and David Edgar, who accepted the challenge of taking one of the most important concepts in modern politics and making it accessible and interesting for anyone, whether you're familiar with the topic or not. As has become key to the Little Black Book series, they've also offered solutions and a clear path forward to save us from the dangers we face before it's too late. I hope you enjoy this important book and please do explore the rest of the series.

Kyle Taylor, creator and executive editor of the Little Black Book series

INTRODUCTION

The rise of the populist right across the globe is already creating dangerous social division and risks increasing discrimination and even violence against women and minorities. To those who still doubt the dangers national populism poses, the first weeks of 2024 were a wake-up call.

In Rome, hundreds of men clad in black gave Mussolini-style salutes outside the former headquarters of the Italian Social Movement (Movimento Sociale Italiano, MSI), the party which has now morphed into the governing Brothers of Italy (FdL).[1]

In the US, ex-president Donald Trump, despite his role in inciting a violent insurrection in January 2021, swept the board in Iowa in the poll to be the Republican candidate for the 2024 presidential election. This result was followed by similar, overwhelming victories across the country.

In the UK, the Sunak government proposed legislation to allow it to deport asylum seekers 4,000 miles to Rwanda with no right of return, even if their asylum claim is shown to be justified. In February 2024, in one of a slew of conspiracist statements, a former Conservative deputy chairman, Lee Anderson, claimed that Islamists had control of the London Mayor.[2]

Meanwhile, the German press revealed that senior officials of Alternative for Germany (AfD), currently running second in national opinion polls, had discussed with other key figures on the European far right plans for the wholesale, compulsory deportation from Germany of migrants and citizens with a foreign background in a scheme reminiscent of Hitler's early plans for Europe's Jews.[3]

Across Europe and beyond, autocrats and strong-arm dictators are on the rise. Former fascists have re-emerged from the shadows; 'post-fascist' parties have sought to sanitise their image; new right-wing populist parties have emerged; some existing conservative parties have been infiltrated and taken over. Now trading under the banner of 'national populism' – the reminted ideology of the populist right – these forces have exploited the failings of the neoliberal establishment and its economic orthodoxies.

National populism focuses on issues of culture, tradition and identity. Demagogues offer a simple but intoxicating narrative, often delivered with charisma and bravado, but with disturbing echoes of pre-war far-right rhetoric.

Mussolini's fascists chanted "God, fatherland and family" ("Dio, patria, e famiglia"), a slogan which prime minister Giorgia Meloni's Brothers of Italy uses today. The Nazis appropriated the imperial German slogan, "Kinder, Küche, Kirche" (children, kitchen, church), while the UK New Conservatives group and national populist champion Matthew Goodwin proclaim the virtues of "faith, flag and family".[4] In a 2017 speech in Warsaw, Donald Trump spoke up for "family, for freedom, for country, and for God".[5]

In addition, national populists have popularised a new lexicon of terms to stigmatise the 'luxury beliefs' and 'virtue signalling' of the 'new elite'. The idea that the 'will of the people' is being frustrated by a 'woke' establishment has been stoked by powerful sections of the press.

National populism shares a number of political characteristics with fascist parties to its right: nationalism, xenophobia, glorification of an idealised national culture, an identified threat from an excluded 'other', an anti-global conspiracy theory and a charismatic leader. However, it has thus far stayed within the mainstream political system, rejected paramilitary organisation, and remained largely non-violent.

This book notes the ideological overlap between national populists and fascists, and recognises that many national populist parties are successors to fascist parties, but we don't think they're the same. Expanding the definition of 'fascism' so widely that it embraces everything unpleasant or dangerous on the right risks our missing the real thing when it emerges or arrives.

In disorienting times of economic hardship and insecurity, national populism's appeal to a traditionalist past strikes a public chord in many countries. In consequence, chunks of the orthodox right have jettisoned their commitment to the values of liberal democracy and are flirting with the hard right, while the main parties of the left have been scrambling to accommodate elements of the national populist agenda, particularly on immigration.

In this book we describe the dismantling of the post-war political settlement, which combined a regulated, civilised capitalism with the welfare state and extensive public ownership, in favour of untrammelled free markets, globalisation and rising inequality. We show how national populists have exploited discontent with the turn towards neoliberal, free-market economics and gained growing public support across Europe and America.

We subject the claims of these parties and their intellectual backers to rigorous scrutiny – with particular reference to the UK – and puncture the fallacies and fantasies that they spread. The book concludes by suggesting how, by working confidently together, people and parties who believe in democracy can rebut this dangerous, anti-democratic onslaught and offer a better future.

European history shows that repression and reaction can be beaten. We hope that this book contributes to the development ' of popular and progressive movements of resistance.

CHAPTER 1

THE BREAK-UP OF THE POST-WWII GLOBAL ORDER

Successful waves of progressive politics have always depended on alliances between different sectors of the population. In the French Revolution of 1789 which ousted the French monarchy, the emerging middle classes needed the help of both the peasantry and urban poor to overthrow the aristocracy. To this day, progressives have needed to bring together a coalition of forces within wider society to mount campaigns for change, win elections and enable reform.

Almost all the great progressive achievements of the 20th century have happened in this way. It took a broad Popular Front of anti-fascist forces and states to defeat Nazism. It took huge popular mobilisations to create the pre-World War Two New Deal in America (which helped bring an end to the Great Depression) and bring about the post-WWII welfare states in Europe, dedicated to preventing the economic misery of the 1930s ever returning.

Large-scale solidarity movements supported the Spanish Republic in its battle against General

Franco's fascists in the 1930s; such movements campaigned against colonialism in the post-war period, and created the civil rights movement which united white, left-wing students with largely Christian black activists in their campaign to desegregate the American South. Many of the same activists – often the children of communist activists of the 1930s and 1940s, the so-called 'red diaper babies' – were part of the global mass movements against US intervention in Vietnam and apartheid in South Africa.

In Britain, Clement Attlee's Labour government of 1945–51 created the National Health Service and nationalised the transport and fuel industries; the Harold Wilson governments of 1964–70 and 1974–76 passed or enabled a raft of landmark social reforms, including the abolition of capital punishment, relaxation of censorship, legalisation of abortion, liberalisation of divorce and decriminalisation of homosexuality, alongside the expansion of comprehensive schools, the establishment of the Open University and the introduction of the Equal Pay and Race Relations Acts. These measures represent a durable package of reforms for which the Wilson governments have received too little historical credit. The reforms of the 1940s and the 1960s were quietly accepted by the Conservative governments which followed.

This alliance between the working class, the growing number of public sector employees and the liberal middle classes that emerged after World War Two ushered in one of the most successful periods in Western history. The French refer to the period between 1945 and 1975 as 'Les Trente Glorieuses', the 30 glorious years. Combining the promotion of economic equality and security with individual freedom, social democratic parties particularly dominated Scandinavian politics and transformed the rest of Europe. Until derailed by the disaster of Vietnam, President Lyndon Johnson, a Democrat, combined civil rights legislation with the massive Great Society programme of welfare reform.

THATCHER AND REAGAN: NATIONAL POPULISM'S FIRST SHOUT

By the mid-70s, then, the post-war alliance between social democrats who believed in greater state intervention in the economy and social liberals who wanted to expand freedoms and justice for women and minority groups was firmly in place across much of the West. Even the nationalist philosopher John Gray (more of him coming later) recognises that "the success story of the post-war world was social democracy". [6]

US president Ronald Reagan and British prime minister Margaret Thatcher changed all that. The 1973 oil crisis, economic stagnation and high inflation gave the new right the opportunity to tear up this post-war settlement and reintroduce a more free-wheeling, laissez-faire model of capitalism. The backlash against social democracy, fuelled by openly discriminatory demagogy, attracted some workers to vote for Thatcher and Reagan on socially conservative issues like racial and sexual equality. Thatcher's policies of council house sales to sitting tenants and offers of shares in privatised industries broadened the Conservative social coalition, giving it new reach into traditionally Labour-supporting working-class communities. In the US, Reagan extended the Republican coalition to embrace born-again Christians (the 'Moral Majority'), conservative white workers (the so-called 'lunch pail Democrats') and even some disillusioned former leftist intellectuals in New York.

Together this new coalition shifted politics decisively to the right and made neoliberalism the new media and establishment orthodoxy, overturning the dominance of interventionist economics based on Maynard Keynes's advocacy of public spending to prevent mass unemployment. The 'Washington consensus' – a cocktail of free markets, privatisation, deregulation and selective small government, required of countries seeking financial assistance from the International Monetary Fund and World Bank – was born. In the process, the post-war, social democratic alliance between economic interventionists and social liberals began to fray.

1989 AND AFTER: THE GLOBALISERS' MOMENT

The collapse of the Berlin Wall and the fall of the Soviet Union continued these trends; 1989 removed the fear of any non-capitalist alternative from the minds of the Western establishment. For many years, left wingers had hoped that without the uninviting example of the USSR, socialism would flourish.

In fact, the reverse happened. Historically, the existence of the USSR fulfilled a paradoxical double role: it discredited socialism while, at the same time, civilising capitalism. Its mere presence had acted as a warning to the right that if they didn't meet some working-class aspirations, another alternative was possible. Without it, the 1990s saw rampant capitalism unchained.

Helped by the brutal consolidation of Deng Xiaoping's state capitalist rule in China, 1989 opened massive new markets to capitalism and gave it a huge boost, not least by hugely expanding the middle class in the developing world. This gave credibility to American commentator Francis Fukayama's thesis that this moment represented "the end of history"; the belief that conflicts between contending classes and ideologies were over; and that the whole world was set on a liberal, capitalist path.

Although this view was most fervently promulgated by fundamentalist free marketers, it was also endorsed by the most senior politicians from the centre and social democratic left. Describing their new policy as a 'Third Way', social democrats like US Democratic president Bill Clinton and Labour leader Tony Blair abandoned the traditional aspirations of their working-class constituents, while continuing to promote social and cultural reform in some areas.

Clinton and Blair dominated the intellectual and political world of the 1990s. The unique global circumstances of the period – the end of the Cold War, the opening of Chinese and ex-Soviet markets to the commercial world and the impact of the information technology revolution – made it possible to believe that capitalism had overcome its inherent problems. Tony Blair's evangelist endorsement of hyperglobalisation was most clearly expressed at Labour's 2005 conference: "I hear people say we have to stop and debate globalisation. You might as well debate whether autumn should follow summer... The character of this changing world is indifferent to tradition. Unforgiving of frailty. No respecter of past reputations. It has no custom and practice. It is replete with opportunities, but they only go to those swift to adapt, open, willing and able to change."[7]

Blair's 'Third Way', with its contemptuous dismissal of the traditional working class as 'old Labour', represented a clear departure from the core beliefs of conventional social democracy. It wasn't a more right-wing version of social democracy but, rather, a clean break from it.

With the economic growth of the 1990s and early 2000s, most social democratic parties in Europe followed the Third Way path. In the UK, this new consensus – both economically and socially liberal – was shared between Blair's New Labour and Nick Clegg's Liberal Democrats and echoed by David Cameron's Conservatives (the second two, of course, forming the 2010–15 coalition government). All three supported free markets; on social issues like gay rights, they were also in lockstep. Having opposed Labour's repeal of Section 28 (the Thatcher-era proscription against 'promoting' homosexuality), David Cameron was to introduce gay marriage in 2014.

NEOLIBERALISM'S NEMESIS: THE 2008 CRASH AND ITS CONSEQUENCES

The financial crisis of 2007–8 left the new economic consensus in tatters. The crash demonstrated that neoliberalism had not escaped the contradictions and crises endemic to capitalism: New Labour and the other Third Way governments had got it wrong. In Britain, New Labour politicians were slow to admit this; while across the European Union (EU) most social democrats remained wedded to the neoliberal orthodoxies embedded in the EU's Maastricht Treaty. This had established the euro, the European Central Bank and the Stability and Growth Pact which set its financial rules and imposed harsh austerity measures on Greece and other southern European states after the crash.

The working class was thus abandoned by traditional social democratic parties at the very moment when profound economic changes were transforming the world of work. Across the industrialised world, the old models of large-scale manufacturing production were rapidly disappearing. The computer IT revolution transformed and still continues to transform labour markets. While it accelerates the concentration of capital, the IT revolution dispersed the traditional concentrations of labour that previously formed the core of the working class (and Marx predicted would prove the gravediggers of capitalism). The iconic shipyards, pits, factories, car plants and steel works that formed the bedrock of the 20th-century labour movement quickly became a shadow of their former selves.

The traditional working class did not completely disappear: it just no longer dominated the labour force. In the UK, 33 million people are economically active, of whom 15.6 million are women and 8.5 million work part time.[8] But it's a fragmented workforce, consisting of the remaining factory workers; a hugely expanded, salaried sector of technical, professional, administrative, supervisory and service employees often referred to as the 'salariat'; a growing number (4.3 million) of self-employed, freelance workers; and an increasingly insecure group at the lower end of the labour market (the 'precariat') working in the unregulated 'gig economy' on zero-hours contracts, without set working hours or guaranteed wages.

This economic transformation was profoundly traumatising for many working-class communities. A sense of alienation and dislocation haunted deindustrialising towns and cities. As trade unions withered and the old cultures associated with work shrank, the parties that had traditionally been the guardians of the labour interest abandoned their historic role. The mass Communist Parties either disintegrated as in France, transformed themselves into US-style Democratic parties as in Italy, or clung to the historic Soviet wreckage as in Greece and Portugal.

In Germany under Gerhard Schroder, the Social Democrats (SPD) followed the 'Third Way' with their 'dritte Mitte' (literally, the third middle), while Blair and co turned their back on 'old Labour'. Even before 2008, wages were stagnating; in the six years following the 2008 crash, real wages for men declined by 7%.[9]

Economically beleaguered, culturally dispossessed and politically abandoned, traditional voters' electoral commitment to Labour slumped: the party lost four million votes, mainly in working-class constituencies, between the 1997 and 2005 elections, and nearly a million more in 2010. Across Europe the working class gazed into a political vacuum. Who would fill it?

CHAPTER 2

NATIONAL POPULISM EMERGES IN MAINLAND EUROPE

—

New political coalitions did not just emerge suddenly after the financial crash of 2008. The alliance between the working class and liberal progressives had been fraying for some time. The Reagan/Thatcher era had paved the way. Yet change was afoot elsewhere too.

This was apparent during the Iranian revolution against the Shah in 1979, where instead of the anti-imperial, revolutionary movement looking to socialist leaders for support, it turned to the resolutely theocratic, anti-modernist leadership of religious fundamentalists.

A similar fracture was apparent during the Arab Spring of 2011. At first, an alliance of the middle classes and the urban and rural poor overthrew autocratic governments across North Africa. Yet with the poor supporting the Muslim Brotherhood, the middle class and intelligentsia retreated from this coalition and enabled the return of military dictatorships in Egypt and elsewhere.

After the anti-communist revolutions of 1989 in eastern Europe, the policies of wholesale privatisation and deregulation imposed by the International Monetary Fund (IMF) and Western advisors were met with enthusiasm by the middle classes and the young, but with fear by workers in smokestack industries facing factory closures and unemployment. These pro-market policies of the mainstream parties were adopted by most ex-communist parties; those who lost out were increasingly attracted to emergent national populism, which played to their economic insecurities and focused on conservative, often religious traditionalism. That rupture has shaped politics across the region ever since.

RUPTURE OF THE CORDON SANITAIRE

In western Europe, the alliance between workers and liberal progressives showed signs of strain but remained broadly intact until the 2008 crash. It was deeply rooted in the traditions that mainstream parties of right and left had followed since the Second World War, and the general acceptance of the French revolutionary principles of liberty, equality and solidarity (first translated as 'fraternity' or 'brotherhood'), with their insistence that freedom and democracy had to have a social dimension.

Alongside the wartime horrors of the Holocaust, the impact of the mass unemployment and widespread poverty of the inter-war period created a new wider commitment to these values across the political spectrum. While some pre-war conservative parties had dallied with fascists and assisted in their rise to power, notably in Germany and Italy, mainstream politicians in the post-war era erected a '*cordon sanitaire*' (defensive barrier), blocking the nationalist and neo-fascist right from any alliance.

This consigned far-right parties whose roots could be traced back to inter-war fascism – including the Italian Social Movement (MSI) and the French National Front (Front National, FN) – to the fringes, and any suggestion that they could join or support governments was deemed beyond the pale.

For most of the post-war era, then, national politics in western Europe has consisted of a sedate, centrist oscillation between conservatives and social democrats. Largely unnoticed by ruling Third Way parties, with the dawn of the new millennium, all that began to change.

THE HARD RIGHT STRIKES BACK

The groupings excluded by the *cordon sanitaire* were of three types. First, there were unashamed neo-fascist parties, including the National Democratic

Party of Germany (Nationaldemokratische Partei Deutschlands, NPD), founded in 1964, and Greece's Golden Dawn (Chrysí Avgí, XA), established in 1980. Although both had limited electoral success – the NPD in state parliaments, Golden Dawn in national elections – neither approached government.

Then there were fascist successor parties, the organisational descendants of pre- or post-war fascist parties, like the Italian Social Movement (MSI) and later the Brothers of Italy (Fratelli d'Italia, FdI), which split from a larger party in 2012; the Austrian Freedom Party (Freiheitliche Partei Österreichs, FPÖ), founded in 1956; and the Sweden Democrats (Sverigedemokraterna, SD), created in 1988.

There were new parties too, some of which began as conventional conservative parties promoting free-market ideologies and then moving rightwards on immigration – like the Norwegian Progesss Party (Fremskrittspartiet, FrP), set up in 1973 and the anti-EU Alternative for Germany (Alternative für Deutschland, AfD), which when formed in 2013 was described as the "party of the professors".[10] Populist parties created specifically to oppose immigration include the Danish People's Party (Dansk Folkeparti, DF), the Finns Party (founded in 1995 as the True Finns, Perussuomalaiset, PS) and the Dutch Freedom Party (Partij voor de Vrijheid, PVV), established in 2006 by Geert Wilders.

Apart from the overt neo-fascists, all these parties sought respectability (some were described as "pinstripe Nazis"). Although they have their differences – particularly on the EU – they share a hostility to immigration and an exclusionary, white nativist approach to nationality.

In seeking mainstream acceptance, many were influenced by the far-right French philosopher Alain de Benoist. Instead of claiming that some races are intrinsically inferior, de Benoist and his followers argued that they are simply different, based on cultural incompatibilities that are given and fixed. Here culture becomes the synonym for race; immigrants are inevitably outsiders as they are carriers of distinct cultures – the other – and can never be absorbed into the host nation.[11] This shift enabled the racist and neo-fascist right to present their arguments in a more palatable form.

Although the key turning point was the crash of 2008, national populists began to achieve significant electoral success earlier, and, in some cases, breached the *cordon sanitaire*. Thus, in 1999, Jorg Haider's fascist successor Freedom Party won 27% of the vote in Austria and became the junior member of a coalition government in early 2000.

In 2001, the Danish People's Party agreed to prop up a conservative-led government; in the same year, in Italy the National Alliance (Alleanza Nazionale,

AN), a successor party to the fascist legacy MSI, was brought into a coalition government led by Silvio Berlusconi; and in 2002, FN founder Jean-Marie Le Pen unexpectedly won a place in the run-off of the French presidential election against the conservative incumbent Jacques Chirac.

AFTER THE CRASH: THE CORDON BREAKS

However, after the financial crisis, as wages stagnated and public services were cut, popular discontent grew. Across mainland Europe, national populist parties were able to fill the gap vacated by a left compromised by its Faustian pact with neoliberalism. Since 2000, in exchange for policy concessions, national populist parties have propped up governments in Denmark, the Netherlands and Sweden, and been part of governing coalitions in Austria, Finland, Italy, Norway, Slovakia and Switzerland, as well as leading governments in Hungary, Italy and Poland. Most recently, Geert Wilders' PVV came first in the 2023 Dutch general election, and Portugal's anti-immigration, anti-Roma party Chega (Enough) quadrupled its parliamentary representation in March 2024. Almost everywhere in mainland Europe national populists are superseding left-wing parties and outstripping the Greens.

Most alarming are national populist advances in the EU's three strongest countries.

In France in 2017 the National Front, renamed the National Rally (Rassemblement National) under the leadership of Marine Le Pen (Jean-Marie's daughter), won 34% of the vote in the presidential election against Emmanuel Macron, with her vote increasing to 41% in a rerun of the contest five years later. Currently, the RN is the main opposition party and well positioned to win the 2027 presidential election.

In Germany, the AfD has benefitted from the dismal economic performance of the three-party governing coalition. Having shifted its principal focus from free-market economics to anti-immigration, and in the wake of significant advances in local and regional elections, the party overtook the ruling Social Democrats in opinion polls in 2023, with the backing of over one-fifth of the electorate. As described in our introduction, in January 2024 it was revealed that AfD leaders had discussed a plan for compulsory deportation of migrants from Germany.

In Italy, following a decade of intermittent rule by charismatic right-wing populists and their parties, from Berlusconi's Forza Italia and Beppe Grillo's Five Star Movement to Matteo Salvini's Lega (formerly the Northern League), or by appointed technocrats such as Mario Draghi, Italy's 2022 general election propelled the leader of the fascist legacy Brothers of Italy, Giorgia Meloni, into the premiership. She has since consolidated her party's electoral support.

National populism's strongest hold on power has been in eastern Europe, where the institutions and practices of liberal democracy were weakest. The IMF's pro-market, shock therapy policies for the region left large swathes of the population in a precarious economic plight and with no political representation. The financial crisis and its aftermath left space for national populists in the Czech Republic and Slovakia to rise to prominence.

In Poland it was the Law and Justice Party (Prawo i Sprawiedliwość, PIS). Founded by former dissident Jarosław Kaczyński as a conventional Christian Democratic party in 2001, the PIS led a coalition government from 2005 to 2007. Moving rightward, the party returned to power in 2015, politicising the civil service and judiciary (leading to protests from the EU), legalising extensive government surveillance and making abortion illegal.[12]

Meanwhile, the Hungarian Fidesz party (an acronym of the Alliance of Young Democrats), founded under communism as a liberal student party, was dragged to the right by its former dissident leader Victor Orban, and has proved the most durable national populist government on the continent. Benefitting from popular disillusionment with the preceding socialist government, Orban was elected as prime minister in 2010, the first of four successive victories. Orban proudly defines his Hungary as an "illiberal democracy",[13] a semi-authoritarian regime which involves – as in Poland – a takeover of the judiciary and much of the media by Fidesz loyalists. Like many national populists, he is opposed to the 'promotion' of homosexuality, seeks to reverse the decline in the Hungarian birth rate, and sees promoting the family and opposing immigration as part of the same project: 'Liberal democracy is pro-immigration, Christian democracy is anti-immigration … while Christian democracy is based on the Christian family model, which is also an illiberal idea'. [14]

In 2019, Orban stated that: "If, in the future, Europe is to be populated by people other than Europeans, then we will effectively be consenting to population replacement", insisting that "there are political forces in Europe who want a replacement of population for ideological or other reasons".[15] Those forces were identified by the Orban government in the text of a demonstrably loaded referendum question put to the nation in 2017, referring to Orban's *bête noire*: "George Soros wants to persuade Brussels to settle at least 1,000,000 people from Africa and the Middle East in European Union territory, including Hungary. Do you support this part of the Soros plan?"[16]

THE NARRATIVE, THE FAULTLINE AND THE CULTURE WAR

The idea that immigration is promoted by sinister international forces for their own secret ends is central to the national populist common narrative, which goes like this:

There is a new, graduate, liberal elite which has seized power in Western countries, in order to promote their own ideological agenda, in the underlying interests of international finance. Undermining the only bulwark against global capital, the nation state, this elite promotes internationalism, the undermining of nations through immigration, and the promotion of liberal values – internationalism, feminism, LGBT+ rights, environmentalism – which demoralise the nation and encourage demographic decline. Finance capital encourages the import of cheap foreign labour, and more generally promotes the interests of ethnic and other minorities against the majority of indigenous white workers. The concept of a conspiracy to replace the white population with what Orban calls "the depth of Africa"[17] – the Great Replacement theory – is a racist formulation promoted by the French intellectual Renaud Camus, whose 2011 book *Le Grand Remplacement* launched the idea.

In order to fight back against the elite, the dominant political faultline of the post-war period must be redrawn. The traditional division pitted (on the right) liberal economics and social conservatism (low taxes and spending; opposition to women's and gay rights and immigration) against (on the left) fairer economics and social liberalism (state intervention in the economy as well as expanding women's and LGBT+ rights and promoting environmental justice and anti-racism).

The new faultline – economic and social liberalism on one side, state interventionism and social conservatism on the other – allows socially conservative workers to vote *for* state intervention and the welfare state and *against* social and cultural liberalism; while it forces people who back both social and economic justice to choose between the two.

To effect this realignment, national populism had to do two things. First, it had to abandon, at least in part, traditional conservative laissez-faire economics. So, parties like Norway's Progress Party and the German AfD ceased to prioritise free-market economics, but shifted their focus to law and order and opposing immigration. Holland's Geert Wilders abandoned his previous opposition both to the minimum wage and to workers' protection against dismissal. When founded, the Austrian Freedom Party wanted to raise the retirement age and reduce family subsidies; the party's 2016 presidential near-winner, Norbert Hofer, rejected the pension age rise and backed the welfare state. Marine Le Pen combines a coherent, anti-migrant nativism with economic and social policies that were once the staple of the left on jobs, the welfare state and opposition to austerity. She refers to the RN as "France's leading working-class party".[18]

Hungary's Orban has combined culturally traditionalist politics with raising the minimum wage, introducing a home-building programme and family subsidies. In Poland, PIS's pro-welfare policies appeal precisely to those working-class and poor rural families who lost out during the free-market 'shock therapy' of the 1990s.[19]

Aside from the move 'left' on economics, the other method of entrenching and fortifying this new faultline is through declaring a culture war against the liberal elite, its training grounds in the universities and the territory it has allegedly captured in the media, the liberal professions and public services. The targets of this war include an independent judiciary, women's and LGBT+ rights, gender ideology, critical race theory, the replacement (or retention) of statues and other memorials, and a more general battle over the teaching and meaning of history.

Overall, national populism has concentrated on the social issues of culture and identity, while moving 'left' on economics in order not to lose socially conservative working-class voters. In Britain, the younger you are, the less likely you are to vote for right or far-right parties. In January 2024, the BBC revealed evidence that this is not the case in mainland

Europe. In the Italian election of October 2022, almost as many voters under 30 voted for Giorgia Meloni as did over-65s. At the last Austrian election, 30% of voters under 30 voted for the Freedom Party, but only 20% of voters over 65. In the 2023 Netherlands election, voters under 35 were more likely to vote for Geert Wilders than voters over 35. And, in the French presidential run-off in 2022, only 30% of voters over 65 voted for Marine le Pen, as against 44% of under 35-year-olds.[20]

There has of course been resistance to the rise of national populism and illiberal democracy. A two-party agreement between the Spanish Socialists and the feminist left, Sumar, held off the challenge from the Popular Party (PP) and hard-right Vox in Spain in July 2023. A three-party coalition with an agreed programme for government managed to dislodge PIS in the Polish election in September of the same year. Following the inconclusive election in March 2024, Portugal's right-wing Democratic Alliance has refused to go into a coalition with the xenophobic Chega Party and will govern as a minority.[21] However, it is clear that the influence of national populists as partners or opponents has dragged the mainstream to the right on cultural issues across the continent.

Ideas and policies which had been consigned to the dustbin of history are defining 21st-century politics across mainland Europe. What has happened in the UK?

CHAPTER 3

WHAT HAPPENED IN THE UK?

The godfather of British national populism was an unlikely choice. Enoch Powell was in one sense anathema to the movement that was to emerge in the early 2000s: he was a fervent, fundamentalist free marketeer who claimed that, when kneeling in church, he would "thank God, the Holy Ghost, for the gift of capitalism".[22] But his hostility to Commonwealth immigration – in his notorious 1968 "rivers of blood" speech and elsewhere – made him an early hero of the constituencies which would later support UKIP, the Brexit Party and post-Brexit Conservatives.

Powell anticipated national populism in many ways: he believed that "the politics of the last few years have been little more than a series of conspiracies conducted by the politicians and the press"; he identified forces aiming at "the actual destruction of our nation and society", from rebellious students to Commonwealth immigrants, whose "accumulation" was "not without deliberate intention".[23] Accordingly, he questioned whether "the Foreign Office was the only Department of State into which enemies of this country were infiltrated".[24]

Following "rivers of blood", Conservative leader Edward Heath expelled Powell from his shadow cabinet, thus placing the man and his ism firmly beyond the *cordon sanitaire*. But, as often happens when mainstream politicians spout racist rhetoric, the immediate beneficiary was the far right. The National Front (NF) had been founded in 1966, by a merger of four existing organisations (the last of which was the openly Nazi Greater Britain Movement). Like the national populists who were to follow, the NF's magazine *Spearhead* asserted that the main threat to the British nation was "international capitalism – a system that has imported foreigners to undercut the wages of British workers and forces us into the Common Market".[25] For the NF's national activities organiser Martin Webster, "the leaders of international finance provide massive financial support both for multi-racialist projects all over the globe and for the support of multi-racialist propaganda"[26] (anticipating Viktor Orban's later accusations against George Soros).

In 1972, the Heath government decided to admit 28,000 British Asians expelled from Uganda by Idi Amin. Protests against this morally correct decision brought the NF into the limelight. By 1974 its membership was estimated at over 100,000. In 1977 it gained 119,000 votes in the London local elections and over 10% of the vote in Leicester and Wolverhampton. The party was also mounting increasingly threatening marches and rallies, at a time when racial violence against Asians in particular was on the rise.

The NF was opposed by propaganda, campaigning and demonstrations organised by the Anti-Nazi League and Rock against Racism, which exposed the NF's origins and turned the tide.

Yet there had long been both a racist and a jingoistic strand within British society, from suburban Conservatives frequenting golf course clubhouses to Labour-supporting London dockers marching in support of Powell in 1968. Many parts of the tabloid press amplified these sentiments. Fearful of being outflanked, Mrs Thatcher gave a television interview on 31 January 1978, openly directed at voters tempted by the NF: "People are really rather afraid that this country might be rather swamped by people with a different culture… we do have to hold out the prospect of an end to immigration".[27] The *cordon sanitaire* was broken.

Alongside the work of the anti-fascist movement, Mrs Thatcher's clear move to the right on immigration contributed to the NF's catastrophic performance in the 1979 general election, winning 0.6% of the national vote. It descended into a whirlpool of angry splits and recriminations.

Meanwhile, within the now ruling Conservative Party, there were challenges to the party's prevailing free market ideology, not just from one-nation Conservatives on the party's left but from the right. Thatcherism was essentially a cocktail of free-market, economic liberalism and an increasingly authoritarian stance against dissent, notably against militant trade unionists, Irish republicans and left-wing Labour councils. The government also promoted socially conservative policies on immigration and sexuality, including the Section 28 criminalisation of 'promoting' homosexuality.

A group of traditionalist Conservatives, many associated with the Cambridge college Peterhouse, had no problem at all with the authoritarianism or the social conservatism, but were deeply concerned about the free-marketeering. In a 1978 collection, *Conservative Essays*, journalist Peregrine Worsthorne poured cold water on the idea of freedom as an essential Conservative value: "The trouble with Labour… is that it has set too many people far too free".[28]

Another *Essays* contributor, the young, former-leftist philosopher Roger Scruton, declared elsewhere that liberalism, economic or social, was no less than "the principal enemy of conservatism", of which democracy itself was not a necessary component.[29] In 1982, Scruton launched the *Salisbury Review*, whose first edition contained an article by fellow

Conservative Essays contributor John Casey, calling for the compulsory repatriation of "the coloured immigrant community".[30] Scruton was to distance himself from the article but not very far: "While we may disagree with the policy of compulsory repatriation… there is no doubt that, merely to arrest the flow of immigrants cannot solve the problem."[31] It was hardly – to put it mildly – a ringing renunciation.

Scruton's antipathy to immigration remained a constant feature; in 2006 he described as "doublethink" the proposition that "pious Muslims from the hinterlands of Asia would produce children loyal to a secular European state… people whose language, customs, and culture mark them out as foreigners".[32] As a forceful critic of free-market economics and proponent of social conservatism, Scruton was to become a key intellectual influence within national populism and beyond.

The British National Party (BNP), the successor to the NF, emerged as an electoral force after the 2001 disturbances in Oldham, Burnley and Bradford. By 2008 it had gained a total of 55 council seats, becoming the second party for a brief period in Burnley and Dagenham. It gained nearly a million votes and two seats in the 2009 European elections, and over half a million votes in the 2010 general election.

To achieve these results, it had followed European post-fascist parties (in the BNP's case, not that 'post') in moderating some policies: it dropped the commitment to compulsory repatriation, and, like many European equivalents, moved left on economics, calling for economic protectionism and some nationalisation. But Britain's electoral system, and its own internal splits and dubious history, limited the BNP's impact. Plus, there was a new kid on the block, untainted by any fascist past.

THE RISE OF UKIP

In 1991, LSE lecturer Alan Sked founded the anti-EU Anti-Federalist League which converted itself into the UK Independence Party (UKIP) in 1993. In the 1997 general election, its 105,722 votes were dwarfed by the 811,849 gained by the maverick millionaire Sir James Goldsmith's Referendum Party. But, following Sked's overthrow later that year – by a faction including Nigel Farage – the party began its steady advance. Eager not to be seen as "the BNP in blazers", UKIP realised that, although many of its voters were indeed in prosperous southern shires,[33] its future didn't lie in being "the Conservative Party in exile".[34]

Under the charismatic leadership of Nigel Farage (2006–2009 and 2010–2016), the party shifted its focus to Labour areas, some of which had been happy hunting grounds for the BNP. The effort to distance

UKIP from the far right was plagued by gaffes by its councillors and MEPs: not for nothing had David Cameron described UKIP's base as "fruitcakes, loonies and closet racists"".[35]

However, it gradually junked many of its dottier proposals and much of its pro-free-market policies while retaining its relentless focus on the twin themes of immigration and the EU. Here it was helped enormously by the repeated discriminatory and sensationalist coverage of ethnic minorities, immigrants and asylum seekers – as well as the EU – that formed the staple diet of much of the Conservative press. *The Daily Express*, for example, ran 22 negative front pages stories about asylum seekers and refugees in a single 31-day period, but it was not alone in its obsessive anti-migrant rhetoric.[36]

In 2014, UKIP came third in Britain's local elections and came first in the European Parliament elections, winning 27% of the Euro vote and 24 MEPs. In the 2015 general election, the party came third, with nearly four million votes. The first past the post system disadvantaged the party electorally but fear of the UKIP threat had led the Conservatives to offer a referendum on EU membership if they won the election.

In 2014, former City metal exchange broker Nigel Farage had declared: "I hate it when I hear this pejorative phrase 'banker'".[37] But, on the morning of 24 June 2016, Farage insisted: "We have fought against the multinationals, we have fought against the big merchant banks".[38] He was referring, of course, to the Leavers' victory in the Brexit referendum.

2016: NATIONAL POPULISM'S 'YEAR OF MIRACLES' (AND AFTER)

Like the rocks exposed by the lowering tide, the referendum exposed the new faultline dividing socially conservative Brexiteers from liberal Remainers. Freed from traditional party contours, working-class electors were able to vote social conservative without having to vote for the rest of the Conservative package as well. As official leader of the Leave campaign, Boris Johnson succeeded in combining blokey, Churchillian rhetoric with the dog-whistle jibes which informed his pre-prime ministerial journalism. His comments about "letterboxes", "bum boys" and "piccaninies with watermelon smiles"[39] served to hearten the hard right, while accusing the EU of "doing the work of Hitler and Napoleon" directly appealed to anti-European nationalists. Although overall, most Brexit voters were southern Conservatives and only a third of 2015 Labour voters voted leave, a majority of Labour constituencies voted for Brexit.

As a result, Theresa May and her advisors hardened their stance on social issues (as home secretary, May had, after all, been in charge of the 'hostile environment' designed to discourage immigrants waiting for leave to stay in the country) while moving their economic rhetoric to the left. In her first speech as prime minister, May promised to be on the side of the "just about managing", and indeed the poor: "If you are from an ordinary working-class family, life is much harder than many people in Westminster realise… The government I lead will be driven not by the interests of the privileged few but by yours".[40]

Three months later, May used her first conference speech to punch some social conservative hot buttons, criticising politicians and commentators who "find your patriotism distasteful, your concerns about immigration parochial, your views about crime illiberal, your attachment to your job security inconvenient". She then pivoted left, pointing out that "it wasn't the wealthy who made the biggest sacrifices after the financial crash but ordinary working-class families". Finally, she whisked both themes into the national populist conspiracy cocktail, attacking "people in positions of power" who behave "as though they have more in common with international elites than with the people down the road, the people they employ, the people they pass in the street. But if you believe you're a citizen of the world, you're a citizen of nowhere".[41]

Claiming to back ordinary people against a faceless, cosmopolitan financial elite, in a pastel form, the British Conservative Party was pushing exactly the same ideology which national populists were promoting across the continent.

Meanwhile, in a distinctly un-pastel form, the same thing was happening to the American Republican Party. After the election of Barack Obama in 2008, hostility to a black president pressurised the Republican Party to move ever rightwards, starting with the rise of the Tea Party movement and then with the successful takeover of the party by Donald Trump. Just as geographer Danny Dorling showed how the crucial votes for Brexit were delivered by Conservative voters in the affluent South,[42] so the 2020 *New York Times* exit poll showed that Biden defeated Trump among the 73% of US voters whose family income was below $100,000, while Trump beat Biden by 11 points among the better off.[43] It was largely richer Americans that nearly won Trump a second term.

But in the same way that it was the one to two million previously politically unengaged working-class voters who swung it for Brexit, so the sliver of support which shifted from Obama to Trump in the northern rustbelt states like Wisconsin and Michigan was a demographic that had suffered acutely in the previous two decades. Between 1998 and 2013, working-class Americans had seen their net worth decline by 53%, as the richest tenth got 75% richer.[44] As Barack Obama had promised to save the auto industry in 2012, Trump had pledged to stop the export of jobs and to put "America first".

Trump began his campaign on 26 June 2015, attacking Mexican immigrants as drug dealers, criminals and rapists. Despite his own widely evidenced sexual proclivities, he presented himself as a born-again social conservative, promising to pack the Supreme Court with judges who would overturn the right to abortion. He also promised policies to protect US industry and its workers and a programme of public works unmatched since the New Deal of the 1930s. As was happening across Europe, a charismatic, maverick political leader was presenting a programme combining interventionist economics with social conservatism, particularly targeting immigration. The difference here was that Trump was not heading a small insurgent political grouping but a major, established political party.

His presidency and its aftermath has been the most profound example to date of the dangers of mainstream parties adopting a national populist agenda. Donald Trump's encouragement of his supporters to storm the Capitol to stop the confirmation of Joe Biden's electoral victory exposed how in thrall the Republican president had become to the anti-democratic, often white supremacist forces that he and his party had unleashed.

Theresa May's pastel populism failed to have the Trump effect. In the 2017 general election, an electorate keen for economic change voted Labour in sufficient numbers to deprive her of David Cameron's 2015 overall majority. Aspects of the result confirmed that the new faultline had been successfully embedded: Labour dramatically increased its vote among Remainers, people with higher levels of education and young people; while the Conservatives won over Leavers, older people, and those with less formal education. So far, so Brexit. But Labour did unexpectedly well because the predicted nuclear winter in its heartlands didn't materialise. With the significant exception of the North-East, every English region swung from the Conservatives to Labour. According to YouGov, Labour won 45% of full-time workers and 44% of part-time;[45] had the vote been confined to people of working age, Jeremy Corbyn would have become prime minister.

In 2019, the story was different. Under Boris Johnson's leadership, with Brexit as the defining issue and liberal one-nation Conservatives purged in parliament, the Conservatives made heavy inroads into 'red wall' Labour territory, and won a substantial majority.

As with other national populists, Johnson's 2019 manifesto promised "opportunity for all", "social justice", raising the minimum wage, nationalising Arriva Rail North and a 'levelling up' agenda for the

North, while he engaged in authoritarian tactics like proroguing parliament. His programme added up to the classic national populist cocktail of economic interventionism and social conservatism.

The ground for this national populist victory had been well laid. Pundits and commentators had been preparing for this moment for years. Five months before Boris Johnson's December 2019 election victory (giving the Conservatives an overall majority of 80 seats) UKIP analyst Matthew Goodwin tweeted to his more than 100,000 Twitter followers that "it is easier for the right to move left on economics than it is for the left to move right on culture".[46] Goodwin had already moved from being an analyst of national populism to being one of its most foremost advocates.

How influential had Goodwin and other ideologues been in embedding the new faultline in British politics, and how important would they continue to be?

CHAPTER 4

BRITISH NATIONAL POPULISM: READY FOR TAKE-OFF

——

As we've seen, the 1980s were a kind of dress rehearsal for the national populism of today. Both Margaret Thatcher's and Ronald Reagan's victories relied on a reconfiguration of the ideological landscape. This change was brought about in America by movements like the Moral Majority and the mass-mail-driven New Right. In Britain, Mrs Thatcher's campaign to push the Conservative Party to the free-market right (then headlined 'monetarism') was aided by campaigns by the anti-union National Association for Freedom (NAFF) but also right-wing think tanks like the free market-promoting Institute for Economic Affairs (IEA) and the Thatcherite Centre for Policy Studies (CPS).

On both sides of the Atlantic, the move rightwards was also steered by former leftists. In America, these included a group of New York intellectuals dubbed the neoconservatives. Led by the movement's 'godfather', the pre-war communist (in fact, Trotskyite) Irving Kristol, the neoconservatives had shifted rightwards because of their alarm at the new left counterculture of the 1960s, and defined themselves, with some irony, as "liberals mugged by reality".[47]

In Britain, prototype Thatcherism was also trumpeted by former communists like novelist Kingsley Amis and former radical commentators like New Statesman editor Paul Johnson. In 2005, Mrs Thatcher insisted that "we could have never defeated socialism" without CPS co-founder Sir Alfred Sherman,[48] who had been a communist and fought on the Republican side in the Spanish Civil War. By 1974, he was insisting that "for the lumpenproletariat, coloured people and the Irish, let's face it, the only way to hold them in check is to have enough well-armed and properly trained police",[49] advice Mrs Thatcher went on to take.

Today's national populists also include a significant number of former leftists who seek to redraw the political and cultural landscape, attributing Boris Johnson's substantial 2019 election victory to the new political configuration, and insisting that the Conservatives must stick to national populist, socially conservative policies.

STRANGE BEDFELLOWS PART 1: RED MEETS BLUE

The construction of this new coalition has encouraged unexpected strange and paradoxical political alliances. The first to appear were the so-called Red Tory and Blue Labour tendencies within the two main political parties, which emerged in the wake of the 2008 crash.

Like many of the traditionalist Conservative ideologues of the 1970s and 1980s, Phillip Blond studied at Peterhouse, Cambridge. He left the centre-left think tank Demos to set up his own, ResPublica, and in 2009 published an article in *Prospect* titled 'Rise of the red Tories',[50] arguing that Conservatives should oppose big business (and the economic liberal values that went with it) while supporting traditionalist social values. Blond was influential on David Cameron's communitarian 'Big Society' initiative.

At around the same time, Labour thinker Maurice Glasman coined the term 'Blue Labour' to describe an equivalent position on the left,[51] again opposed to capitalism but also emphasising the principles of 'faith, flag and family'.[52] In support of Blue Labour, its advocate Jonathan Rutherford declared that, 'Labour's future is conservative'.[53] Glasman was ennobled by Labour leader Ed Miliband; of the problems of the Blue Labour brand, more later.

Even stranger than the Red Tory/Blue Labour double act, however, is the ideological overlap between Spiked, the website of a formerly Marxist, now individualistic right libertarian campaign group, and Unherd, the main online home of anti-liberal communitarianism, focused on the assumed, unchanging pillars of the traditional family and nationhood. So how on earth – on most of the major social issues of the day – do these two publications appear to be marching in lockstep?

STRANGE BEDFELLOWS PART 2:
SPIKED AND UNHERD

Both Spiked and Unherd are prolific websites supplying a daily flow of political and cultural commentary. The former is an outgrowth of the Revolutionary Communist Party (RCP), which developed an increasingly eccentric version of Trotskyism through its magazine *Living Marxism*, which, among other obviously Marxist preoccupations, campaigned against gun control and for global warming and the advertising of tobacco.[54] It was successfully sued by ITN for alleging that pictures of a Bosnian concentration camp were faked, and the party wound itself up in 1998.[55] In 2000, a number of members of the now defunct RCP launched the webzine *Spiked*. Its cadres and supporters – including guru Frank Furedi, polemicist and now Brexit-supporting peer Claire Fox, and Boris Johnson's ex-policy chief Munira Mirza – continued the RCP's trajectory towards anti-statist, economic libertarianism. The group nonetheless retained both its original Leninist discipline, and its capacity for harsh polemic.

Unherd has more conventional origins within the Conservative party. Harking back to the free market-sceptic *Conservative Essays* of the early 1980s, Unherd's 2017 founder Tim Montgomerie described his, Unherd's and national populism's mission in a crucial, defining phrase: he argued for a "social Thatcherism", which would rebalance "from a conservatism of freedom to a conservatism of locality and security"; he went on to claim that, within the Conservative Party, "the magnetism of national sovereignty has finally overtaken the magnetism of free markets".[56] Unherd's many polemicists include the ex-Socialist Workers Party-flirting vicar Giles Fraser and fire union member Paul Embery, whose 2020 anti-woke polemic[57] added him to a growing list of pundits who happily write both for the right libertarian Spiked and the communitarian Unherd.

The reason for this unexpected cross-fertilisation of ex-Trotskyites and traditionalist Conservatives is explained by their shared ideological commitment to Brexit, but also their vitriolic hostility to the left from which Spiked grew and the new social movements – feminism, LGBT+ rights, environmentalism, anti-racism – that found such success over the last decades.

The two websites cover a broad spread of topics and Unherd especially attracts a wide range of authors. Its line-up of regular columnists demonstrates its national populist, communitarian and culture warrior proclivities, as does Spiked's. A typical (June 2022) Spiked home page advertised articles on 'Why gun control is racist', 'Why Jamie Oliver can BOGOF', 'The cultural imperialism of taking the knee' and why 'a woke police force is the last thing we need'.

Neither website is short of funds. Both receive hefty support from key figures associated with the populist right. Unherd is funded by an endowment from Sir Paul Marshall, a senior hedge fund manager and ardent supporter of Brexit. He gave £500,000 to the Conservative Party in 2019 and is a major funder of, and for a short period chaired, GB News.[58] Spiked's funding sources include $300,000 from the Charles Koch Foundation to Spiked's American arm.[59] The Koch brothers have been among the most substantial funders of Donald Trump.

These websites are the intellectual outriders for national populism. Both have significant readerships. But their main impact is the way their ideas – particularly on multiculturalism and the 'woke agenda' – have been eagerly lapped up by the mainstream right-wing media. Unherd editor Freddie Sayers wrote a set of columns in the *Daily Telegraph* throughout the COVID crisis attacking lockdowns, while Spiked deputy editor Ella Whelan also writes regularly for the *Telegraph,* largely on the so-called culture wars. Mick Hume, former editor of *Living Marxism* and then of *Spiked*, had a decade-long stint with *The Times*, as well as blasting off occasional polemics in *The Sun* and now enjoying a regular slot in the *Daily Mail*. After the collapse of the Truss government, former revolutionary Hume wrote an article for the *Mail* calling for the immediate re-election of Boris Johnson.[60]

Indeed, the *Mail* plays a pivotal role in the dissemination of this agenda, no doubt helped by the presence of Jacob Furedi, son of Frank, as its features editor until 2022, when he moved to become associate editor at Unherd. *Spiked's* chief political writer Brendan O'Neill is a daytime TV regular, as is Whelan. At times these pundits have direct connections to government, most notably when Munira Mirza served as Boris Johnson's head of policy.

According to research published by the Institute of Race Relations' journal *Race & Class*, 12 of Spiked's authors have written for the *Telegraph*, nine for the *Mail,* eight for *The Times*, four for *The Sun* and one for the *Express*. Despite attacking the BBC for being 'systematically' woke, Spiked authors have appeared no less than 57 times on *Question Time*, as well as frequently on *BBC Politics Live*, *Newsnight*, *Any Questions* and *The Moral Maze*.[61] As authors Huw C. Davies and Sheena E. Macrae put it, the Spiked community "is subsidised by private donors and offshored capital, has permanent seats in the House of Lords, has a significant media presence reaching an audience of millions, operates within influential think tanks, and has open access to the party of government. Yet it claims to be external to the elite".[62]

Despite their ideologies being logically contradictory, the individualistic libertarians of Spiked and the communalist conservatives of Unherd agree on three of the major issues of the day: climate, feminism and race.

THE IDEOLOGICAL OVERLAP: CLIMATE, FEMINISM AND RACE

In the run-up to the Glasgow international climate change conference in November 2021, COP26, both Spiked and Unherd ran material unremittingly hostile to the entire climate change agenda, each running pieces by the same US author denying the existence of any problem. Michael Shellenberger's Unherd piece 'Climate change is no catastrophe' blithely claimed that a global temperature rise of 3°C would be no big deal.[63] He followed this piece several days later with an interview in Spiked where he maintained that "using gas and nuclear is really all that matters on climate change".[64]

At root, Spiked and Brendan O'Neill (Shellenberger's interviewer) believe in unrestrained economic growth and see any movement that checks or places conditions on that growth as a negative influence that undermines capitalism. In his view, environmentalism is "the revenge of the aristocracy against modernity".[65] As a result, as of July 2022, Spiked had 637 negative mentions of net zero on its website.[66]

A second key battleground is feminism. Unherd has plenty of female writers. At times it recognises the women's movement and sometimes uses its language. Yet one of its main female staff writers, Mary Harrington, demonstrates Unherd's opposition to modern feminism. Harrington's long essay 'The sexual revolution killed feminism' echoes the standard right-wing trope that "feminism today is mainly driven by bourgeois white American women… and serves their class interests".[67]

Bewilderingly, Harrington argues that "modern feminism ended in the 1960s, killed by the twin technology shocks of contraception and abortion" and claims it has now "moved into a radical, individualistic bio-libertarianism".[68] This is an attempt to empty feminism of its substantive content as a collective movement created to address the structural inequalities that women experience in their everyday lives, and which mobilised women to campaign for equal pay, girls' education, contraception, abortion and safety, with great success.

But then Harrington doesn't believe in patriarchy, which she caricatures as a belief in "an eternal conspiracy against women". Instead, she cites the traditionalist thought of the American arch-Republican campaigner Phyllis Schlafly and calls for '"an older relational feminism that can make common cause with conservatives".[69] A clue as to its precise content comes in her piece 'The feminist case against abortion'[70] and Paul Embery's calls for Labour to make the return of the family wage – i.e., putting women back in the home – as a mainstay of its economic policy.[71] Similarly, jabs at contemporary feminism in Spiked include Brendan O'Neill on the alleged "crisis of feminism"[72] and Ella Whelan insisting that "International Women's Day is about everything but women".[73]

The disdain for addressing the structural inequalities that shape women's lives fits with the obsessive attacks on Black Lives Matter and anti-racist movements. George Floyd's death in Minneapolis in May 2020 at the hands of a white policeman sparked the largest protests ever against racial injustice in the United States and across the world. In response, Unherd argued that white support for BLM was just a matter of assuaging white guilt. In Spiked, we read the same argument.[74]

More generally, both sites either deny or downgrade the extent of racial discrimination and inequalities. They shared the joy with which the right-wing commentariat greeted the UK government's 2021 report on racial disparities (The Report of the Commission on Race and Ethnic Disparities, CRED),[75] established under the tutelage of Munira Mirza and chaired by black consultant Tony Sewell, which minimised the extent of racial discrimination in the UK. Its existence is not hard to find. In April 2023, the Race Equality Foundation's investigation into racism and ethnic inequality revealed that one in six people from minority groups had been physically assaulted, more than a quarter had experienced racial insults, and nearly a third suffered discrimination in education and housing.[76] Discrimination against people of colour in the criminal justice system is proverbial. The government's own figures record that in the year ending March 2023, people identifying as black or black British were searched at a rate 4.1 times higher than those from a white ethnic group across England and Wales.[77] Similarly, COVID-19 exposed the dramatic differences in health outcomes between the white majority and black people.[78]

Spiked's effusive response to the Sewell report – 'The life chances of ethnic-minority Britons are not determined by racism. Why is it verboten to say this?' – demonstrated the website's new-found attachment to communitarianism: "Sewell's report... emphasised many often overlooked factors that shape the life chances and personal development of ethnic-minority Britons – such as family structure, which tragically continues to be ignored as an issue in British politics."[79]

In the early days of Spiked, there was still an acknowledgment of institutional racism.[80] But more recently, Spiked writers have changed tack. Brendan O'Neill welcomed the Sewell report's assertion that the term 'institutional racism' was being "liberally used", often "without evidence", as a sign that the "myth" of institutional racism was collapsing.[81]

Meanwhile, among several pro-Sewell articles In Unherd, Eric Kaufmann (author of *Whiteshift*) parcelled the issue up with an attack on woke, asserting that the report "strikes a major blow against institutional wokeness" by "repudiating the grievance-based meta-narrative that has defined this institutional space".[82]

So, then, on three of the great social issues of our era, Spiked and Unherd deploy similar arguments and even phraseology, to minimise the issues or to deny that there's a problem at all. After the premeditated murder of 10 people by an 18-year-old white supremacist in Buffalo in May 2022, Somali-born activist Aysan Hirsi Ali asserted in Unherd that systemic racism is exaggerated: "despite the fact that some racism does still persist, America remains the best country in the world to be black."[83]

THE FOUR Gs

In addition to the former Trotskyites of *Spiked* and the Red Tories of *Unherd*, the most prominent and prolific proponents of the national populist agenda are an academic, a commentator, a political thinker and a philosopher, three of whom were on the left, and whose names conveniently begin with the same letter. The academic is Matthew Goodwin, Professor of Politics at the University of Kent, who describes how he sees his role as follows:

"You don't need a mass movement to win the culture wars. You don't need a new political party. What you need is what we would call an SAS. You need a special force of a small number of highly committed disciplined serious people including academics, lawyers, advisors, campaigners, and you basically need to focus in a laser-like way on the issue at hand."[84]

The above faux-Leninist proposal comes from, as Goodwin admits, a former "fully paid-up member of the liberal left".[85] He is now a pin-up boy of the populist right, who complains about the exclusion of national populist ideas from popular discourse in the *Express*, *Mail*, *Times*, *Sunday Times*, *Telegraph* and *Sun*.

In less than a decade he has shifted from describing to promoting national populist ideas. In 2014, his and Robert Ford's insightful *Revolt on the Right* revealed the increasing purchase of UKIP among working-class voters.[86] In *National Populism: The Revolt against Liberal Democracy*, written with Roger Eatwell in 2018, national populist concerns were "both real and legitimate".[87] By his latest, relentlessly self-promoted "Values, voice and virtue', Goodwin is clearly advocating the ideology he started out just exposing.

Speaking to the National Conservatism (NatCon) Conference in May 2023, Goodwin asserted that the Conservative party had squandered a "historic opportunity to realign its electorate",[88] along the new political faultline that won Brexit and the 2019 election, which he has elsewhere described as meeting voters "on both the cultural axis, defending faith, flag and family, and the economic axis, speaking to voters who are sick and tired of being battered by the winds of globalisation".[89] The key task for the Goodwin SAS is to embed this new faultline in a narrative built round the idea that "a new and deeply narcissistic elite minority"[90] is running – and ruining – the nation.

In near lockstep with Goodwin marches the former youthful Marxist David Goodhart, also a NatCon speaker and *Mail* columnist, who founded the liberal left *Prospect* magazine, went on to head Demos and is now 'Head of Demography, Immigration and Integration' at the right-wing think tank Policy Exchange.

The third G is Maurice Glasman, founder and guru of Blue Labour, who was ennobled on the recommendation of Ed Miliband in 2011, and immediately argued for a halt to immigration and for dialogue with the English Defence League.

And fourth is John Gray, a bleak, nationalist philosopher, hostile to the Enlightenment and any idea of human progress, who is currently spending much of his energy attacking the green movement.

All four Gs have written for Unherd and both Goodwin and Glasman for Spiked (in 2022, Spiked ran long extracts from Glasman's latest book, *Blue Labour: the Politics of the Common Good*).[91] Glasman, Goodhart and Goodwin were all signatories of the anti-EU 'Full Brexit' statement. Gray's main outlet is the increasingly post-liberal *New Statesman* with its accounts of great power rivalry, resource scarcity and the crumbling of the liberal rules-based order themed under the umbrella of "the new age of tragedy".[92]

THE NEW (LIBERAL, GLOBAL, METROPOLITAN, COSMOPOLITAN, ETC.) ELITE

Central to the national populist narrative is the concept of the all-powerful liberal elite allegedly running Britain. For both Goodwin and Goodhart, the elite is a two-headed monster. In the Goodhart version the permissive, let-it-all-hang out 1960s –

with its attacks on "traditional forms of family life" and its liking for human rights and immigration – was nonetheless a "close cousin" of the harsh economic individualism of the Thatcher years.[93]

For Goodwin, it all went wrong not in 1997 but in 1979: the enemy is both economically liberal Thatcherism and socially liberal Blairism. Thus he argues that much of the "radical economic liberalism of the 1980s" was embraced by Tony Blair's New Labour, on to which was grafted "a radical cultural liberalism".[94] It was this "new and narrow orthodoxy of economic and social liberalism which reflected the outlook of the new elite",[95] now no less than "a new ruling class" of middle-class graduates, enjoying "dominance over the commanding heights of British society".[96]

The result has been a deep fissure in society which national populism is beginning to answer. In his 2017 *The Road to Somewhere*, Goodhart argues that this "backlash" speaks to ordinary people "displaced by a more open, ethnically fluid, graduate-favouring economy and society, designed by and for the new elites".[97] The book proposes a sociological distinction between internationalist, liberal, metropolitan 'anywhere' people, particularly concentrated in the "insecure, congested, transit camp" that is London,[98] and the majority 'somewhere' people with their preference for place, stability and nation. Goodhart calculates the conservative somewhere people at half the population and the liberal anywheres at about a quarter with a class of "in-betweeners" making up the rest.[99]

For Gray, the target is, variously, "the liberal political class" and "liberal elites",[100] "the progressive bourgeoisie"[101] and "alt-liberals".[102] For Maurice Glasman, Labour "is stuck in a globalized and liberal vision of the future, which has rendered it incapable of understanding itself or the country".[103] An all-powerful New Elite that represents about one in four of the population is also identified in Matthew Goodwin's *Values, Voice and Virtue*, a book which, the author modestly claims, will resonate "across the globe".[104]

And what is the aim of this New Elite? In the book, Goodwin doesn't say, beyond the generality that the elite wishes to push through "a revolution which reflects their values, interests and priorities".[105]

Elsewhere, however, he advances the national populist, conspiratorial argument that what John Gray calls "woke insurgents"[106] don't just believe the same things, but are actually acting in alliance with international big business. The main evidence for the idea is the syndrome dubbed 'woke capitalism', in which companies – usually retail ones, like supermarket chains – support liberal initiatives like Black History Month and taking the knee. In fact, the impetus for companies supporting a progressive agenda comes from below: in a *New York Times* article Ross Douthat acknowledges that companies' support for liberal causes – airlines and car rental companies dissociating from the gun lobby, for example – is prodded by "their own idealistic young employees"[107] as well as their own self-interest in appealing to customers.

Quite properly, Matthew Goodwin berates Sainsbury's for paying its CEO £4m and handing on its rate relief to shareholders (as Goodwin concludes: "But, hey, go woke capitalism!").[108] But he has a deeper purpose, to support the national populist thesis that his "liberal elite" is working together with international capitalism, in a plot of which immigration is a part. So, in the *Daily Mail*, Goodwin argues that "multinational firms" are 'indulging in 'woke capitalism' whereby they voice strong support for the new belief system while doing all they can to avoid paying a fair share of tax and doing more for their working-class employees. The end result is a sort of informal alliance between white elites, corporations and minorities against the white working class".[109] Thus blatantly ignoring the fact that many of Sainsbury's employees are black, Asian or mixed race.

Goodwin is well aware that, in this argument, he is supporting a conspiracy theory which alleges that global financial elites are using immigration as a means of undermining nation states, as the National

Front argued in the 1970s. In his and Roger Eatwell's *National Populism*, Goodwin describes the Hungarian version of the aims and objectives of the New Elite – particularly with regard to immigration: "Elsewhere in Europe, national populists like Hungary's Viktor Orban argue that liberal politicians within the EU, along with the billionaire Hungarian-Jewish financier George Soros, are engaged in a plot to flood Hungary and 'Christian' Europe with Muslim immigrants and refugees, which they see as part of a quest to dismantle Western nations and usher in a borderless world that is subservient to capitalism".

On the next page, Goodwin and his co-author assert that some of these claims are "not entirely without credence". [110]

AGAINST CULTURAL MODERNITY: IMMIGRATION, DEMOGRAPHICS, CLIMATE AND UNIVERSITIES

These attempts to ally progressive graduates with big business are complemented by a relentlessly anti-modern cultural story. Each form of national populism has its own distinctive mix of nostalgia, family and religion: in Hungary and Poland there is a religious focus on the nuclear family and hostility to LGBT+ rights; it's similar with Italy's Meloni; in US the emphasis is on abortion. In the UK the emphases revolve around a cultural nostalgia for an age when women stayed at home, Britain ruled an empire and universities were the preserve of the few. And people were white.

We have seen how central the issue of race is to national populism in Europe and America. In Britain, David Goodhart led the charge. As early as 2004, he argued in *Prospect* that diversity and solidarity were incompatible because "to put it bluntly, most of us prefer our own kind".[111] Two years later, in a Demos pamphlet called 'Progressive nationalism', he argued for banning veiled women from public buildings, alongside a two-tier welfare system, the teaching of imperial history in schools and the reintroduction of national service.[112]

Echoing Alain de Benoist's argument, Goodhart claimed in *The British Dream* (2013) that the issue with immigration is not economic but cultural: a "meaningful" community "excludes as well as includes".[113] So, even where "racism is racism", it is not so much about colour prejudice, but "what skin colour or distinctive dress represent in terms of different values or behaviours or traditions and the challenge they present to mainstream norms".[114]

Hence, Goodhart's insistence in 2018 that the Windrush scandal "must not lead to a radical watering down of the 'hostile environment'".[115]

In April 2011, the newly ennobled Maurice Glasman suggested that immigration "undermined solidarity, it undermines relationships, and in the scale that it's been going on in England, it can undermine the possibility of politics entirely". A week later he suggested talking to the English Defence League, and on 18 July he told the *Daily Telegraph* that "Britain is not an outpost of the UN. We have to put the people in this country first". Asked if that meant a stop to immigration, Glasman answered "yes".[116] It should be said that, following Glasman's statement, a number of Blue Labour supporters announced that they no longer wished to be associated with the tendency, and Glasman later admitted that his three 2011 interviews betrayed "crassness and thoughtlessness".[117]

For Matthew Goodwin, cultural opposition to immigration has become an ever-increasing preoccupation.

In 2023, he argued that support for immigration is one of a number of "luxury beliefs" held by his New Elite, who are "rapidly eroding the shared history, national identity, culture and symbols, such as cricket, which the majority cherish".[118] On 31 August 2023, he posted a Substack titled 'What I told a cabinet minister', claiming that the government had been encouraged by a "Charity-Judicial Industrial Complex" to leave millions "with a palpable sense that the country they love, the culture, traditions, and ways of life they love, are being completely reshaped" by mass immigration.[119]

Following in Orban's footsteps, Goodwin is also one of a number of national populists who are foregrounding an alleged demographic danger. In a June 2023 tweet, he cited a report on the decline of Britain's birth rate which was also used by evangelical Christian Conservative MP Miriam Cates in a striking speech at the NatCon conference, where she claimed that the "overwhelming threat to British conservatism and, indeed, the whole of Western society" was a decline in the domestic birth rate.[120] Like Goodwin, she wants to reduce immigration dramatically.

As we have seen, fear of demographic decline, associated with hostility to immigration, are the twin pillars of the Great Replacement theory, promoted by national populists as part of the alleged conspiracy by global financial powers to destroy nation states.

We have already pointed out how both Spiked and Unherd used the Glasgow COP26 to challenge the climate change agenda. Two of the four Gs have joined in the attack. Describing the Green New Deal as an "illusion" and an example of "bourgeois environmentalism", John Gray attacks "the dangerous conceits of the green revolution".[121]

Matthew Goodwin, too, claims climate change for the woke agenda, advising Rishi Sunak to tell voters that "We need to help people get through the current crisis by slashing Net Zero costs and, while we're at it, other unnecessary and costly woke policies like diversity, equity, and inclusion programmes".[122]

For national populist conspiratorialists, the green movement is part of a 'Great Reset' plot, conceived at Davos and launched in 2020, to use lockdown and the greening of the economy to bring about an authoritarian, socialist world government.[123]

National populist ideologues have another target. As most New Elitists are graduates, it's no surprise that national populists would like to reduce the size – and thereby influence – of the institutions which produce them. In *The Road to Somewhere*, David Goodhart declared that the university sector "has expanded far beyond any useful purpose";[124] his 2020 book *Head Hand Heart* consists of a sustained attack on the expansion of universities, which has led to "the takeover of politics by an educated elite", tending "to pursue its own interests and intuitions",[125] including, of course, support for immigration.

Similarly, John Gray criticises the "over-enlarging of the university system", not least because it has led to "progressivism" becoming "the unthinking faith of millions of graduates", universities now being, of course, "centres of censorship and indoctrination".[126]

Others are keen to promote part or all of the national populist programme through Spiked, Unherd and the mainstream media. Firefighters union activist Paul Embery, who writes for both websites, is a fervent critic of woke capitalism, and divides the nation – tellingly – into "a rootless, cosmopolitan, bohemian middle-class" and "a rooted, communitarian, patriotic working-class".[127] The starting point of Eric Kaufmann's book *Whiteshift* is that white identity is not "a fabrication designed to maintain power", but "an ethnic identity like any other", under threat from "the anti-white ideology of the cultural left".[128]

BRITISH NATIONAL POPULISM GOES GLOBAL

British national populists are part of a growing, international national populist alliance. Very regular Spiked contributor Frank Furedi, formerly ideological leader of the Revolutionary Communist Party, has addressed the US-based Conservative Political Action Conference's Budapest gathering and is now the executive director of the Mathias Corvinus Collegium (MCC), a Brussels-based private college financed by the Hungarian government to promote Orban and Orbanism in the West.[129]

In addition to its Brussels activities, MCC also operates in London, by favour of the Roger Scruton Legacy Foundation. Scruton had form on supporting the far right in Europe: in 2006 he told a meeting of the far-right Flemish nationalist Vlaams Belang (Flemish Interest, VB) that immigration and the EU would destroy Flanders.[130] In 2019, Scruton was awarded the Hungarian Order of Merit by Viktor Orban for "foreseeing the threats of illegal migration and defending Hungary from unjust criticism".[131] In the same year, Scruton was dismissed from the chairmanship of Britain's Building Better Beautiful Commission, following an interview in the *New Statesman* in which he supported two load-bearing pillars of Viktor Orban's conspiracy theory, the "sudden invasion" of Hungary by "huge tribes of Muslims", and its alleged cause: "Anyone who doesn't think that there is a Soros empire in Hungary has not observed the facts".[132]

So popular is Scruton among the fascist successor Sweden Democrats and its chief ideologue Matthias Karlsson ("Scruton has been my inspiration!") that its youth wing goes around sporting 'Sir Roger Scruton' T-shirts.[133] Scruton is also cited as a major influence by Blue Labour's Jonathan Rutherford and Maurice Glasman, Suella Braverman and no less than two prime ministers.

'WHO DARES WINS': THE IMPACT OF GOODWIN'S SAS

We've seen how national populist culture warriors appeal to the Conservative press and Conservative politicians. Since the financial crisis they have become an increasingly dominant influence on

Conservative and wider British politics. David Goodhart's 'somewhere/anywhere' formulation clearly influenced Theresa May's "citizens of nowhere" speech. The speech's co-author Nick Timothy summed up the 4G thesis as follows: "In reality, most voters want Britain to become more culturally conservative – cutting immigration, cutting crime, and getting on with Brexit – and they want more intervention in the economy", taking on crony capitalists and stopping "wealth consolidating in the hands of a privileged few".[134] John Gray's pithier summation of the same thought was that "Britain needs a Conservative Party that prizes social cohesion over economic expansion".[135]

The impact has continued to be felt. In her 2023 Conservative Party speech, then home secretary Suella Braverman used the national populist coinage "luxury beliefs" to berate anti-racist campaigners.[136] According to Goodwin, his book interested Braverman and her team so much "they asked to meet me".[137]; in January 2024, Goodwin headlined an event he attended addressed by the prime minister as 'My night with Rishi'.[138] However self-inflated, Goodwin and his allies have popularised or created a whole new language of politics – woke, blob, new elite, luxury beliefs, cultural Marxism, citizen of nowhere, virtue signalling – which litters the pages of the Conservative press and speeches of Conservative politicians.

And in all the areas where national populist intellectuals have led the way, Rishi Sunak has followed.

During the summer 2022 Conservative leadership election campaign between Rishi Sunak and Liz Truss, Sunak declared that he had "zero interest in fighting a so-called culture war".[139] Nonetheless, facing defeat, the allegedly social liberal Sunak turned on the "lefty woke culture that is trying to cancel our history, our value and indeed our women",[140] whether by "pulling down statues of historic figures" or "replacing the school curriculum with anti-British propaganda".[141] As prime minister, he focused on refugees and asylum seekers, nationalism and crime, as well as reneging on his climate change commitments.

And then, in December 2023, Sunak attended a right-wing festival in Rome, organised by the fascist successor Brothers of Italy (FdL), thus further blurring the lines between former fascists and traditional conservatives.[142] Sunak and the FdL prime minister Giorgia Meloni's declared friendship is based on a shared love of fantasy literature, the works of J.R.R. Tolkein (as a child, Meloni enjoyed dressing up as a hobbit)[143] and – yes, again – Roger Scruton, described by Meloni as the single greatest influence on her party.[144]

'WHATEVER IS NECESSARY'

The Four Gs and their Spiked and Unherd outriders do not all believe the same things. But they all give credence to the core national populist contention that the country is being run by a liberal elite; all see Brexit as a great opportunity for a renewed UK; while Goodwin believes that the liberal elite is conspiring with multinational companies and minorities to do down the white working class. Goodwin increasingly sees himself as the commander of a crack SAS spearhead, leading his serious, disciplined warriors into battle and continuing to influence the highest levels of government.

On 16 August 2023, his Substack advocated the creation of a New Party, whose Trumpian five-point policy platform would be crime ("get serious about tackling it"), immigration ("do WHATEVER IS NECESSARY"), woke political correctness ("strip it all out"), identity ("promote Britain's distinctive identity, culture and history") and "economic populism" (attacking "big global corporates", "systematic tax avoidance" and "obscene executive pay").[145] In January 2024 he called on Rishi Sunak to put a referendum on reducing immigration in the Conservative manifesto.[146]

Just over a month later, on 1 March 2024, the prime minister delivered his "address on extremism" outside 10 Downing Street. Sunak was careful to avoid generalised anti-Muslim rhetoric, and praised Britain's "multi-ethnic, multi-faith democracy". But he also claimed that democracy was "being deliberately undermined" by "forces here at home trying to tear us apart", calling for such forces to be excluded from civic life, demanding that universities "stop extremist activity on campus", insisting on firmer policing of demonstrations, and threatening the deportation of visa-holding protestors who "spew hate".[147] On 13 March, he refused to commit to returning £10m to a Conservative donor alleged to have said that Diane Abbott MP should be shot.

Praising Sunak's Downing Street speech ("it's high time somebody in our ruling class gets serious about the threats we face") Matthew Goodwin proposed a programme of policies "our ruling class" should immediately implement, including deporting "foreign nationals who glorify Islamist terrorism without appeal", rejecting the concept of "Islamophobia", ending mass immigration, reversing multiculturalism, closing down television channels and charities perceived to advocate extremism, forcing all newcomers to "learn our language, values, history, and ways of life", and pushing back against "radical woke ideology".[148]

To date these national populist culture warriors have been very successful in transforming the tone and terms of political debate. They are increasingly dominating the political and cultural landscape with their populist lexicon, reshaping and reframing the language of politics. In the process they are dragging politics way to the right. Yet their core story is fatally flawed.

CHAPTER 5

FATAL FLAWS

———

As we've seen, national populism is based on a theory of the world which shapes the beliefs and actions of its actual and potential supporters. In its most complete form, the theory asserts that a new liberal elite is acting in cahoots with global financial powers to undermine nation states through the demoralisation and replacement of the indigenous population via demographic decline and immigration.

The only force able to combat this is the majority population, which holds on to traditionalist, conservative opinions and is fighting back.

This theory is wrong on all counts. Firstly, in the form in which national populists promulgate it, the liberal elite doesn't exist. Secondly, in Britain (and many other countries) the majority is moving in a more, not less, liberal direction. And thirdly, the conspiracy claims are not only fantastical but echo dangerously toxic theories from the 20th century.

THE NEW ELITE FANTASY

The most complete summation of the new elite theory is in Matthew Goodwin's much self-touted 'values, voice and virtue'. Goodwin is right that graduates tend to be more liberal than the rest of the population. But central to this theory is the idea that they are also in alliance with global financial capital. Does that stand up?

David Goodhart and Matthew Goodwin agree on the extent of the new elite. Goodhart's 'anywhere' people are about a quarter of the population;[149] Goodwin's 'new elite' are also around 25%, "held together by their university degrees from one of the prestigious Oxbridge or Russell Group universities".[150] In fact, Oxford and Cambridge are part of the Russell Group, whose graduates represent only 6% of the working population.[151] For Goodwin, the elite oscillates between the Russell Group and the whole graduate population, depending on his argument at the time.

Goodwin's frequent lists of the beliefs of the New Elite betray similar inconsistencies. Obviously, the elite takes a "liberal cosmopolitan and progressive world view",[152] supporting "abortion, homosexuality, casual sex, prostitution, divorce, gender equality and immigration".[153] But it's vital to his theory that the elite are also "more economically liberal",[154] more "likely to view the world through an individualist lens" rather than prioritising "collective, group-based attachments",[155] more in favour of open markets and "least concerned about rising inequality".[156]

In other words, for Goodwin and Goodhart – who calls this ideology "double liberalism" – the New Elite supports both economic *and* social liberalism, Thatcherism *and* Blairism. Both claim that a quarter of the population are social liberals who also support the ideas and interests of global big business.

The idea that finance capitalists and university graduates share a common belief system is belied by Goodwin's own calculations. In one of his many tables, Goodwin cites research which calculates "radical progressives" – or, as he quotes John Gray describing them, "hyper-liberals" – as 13% of the population, and thus fully half the New Elite. (For some sociologists, we're told, this segment is even higher, up to 23% of the population.)[157]

Are these "radical progressives" really latter-day Thatcherites who like open markets and want more inequality? Are they hell. Indeed, the claim is strongly disputed by Goodwin's own data. As we might expect, in reality this radical progressive group leans "strongly to the left in politics", is "strongly motivated by the pursuit of social justice", and is most likely to believe that people's outcomes "are defined more by social forces than by individual responsibility". The progressives also "elevate the group over the individual".[158]

In other words, *at least half* of Goodwin's notional New Elite are politically opposed to the Thatcherite, neoliberal economics which Goodwin claims they advocate and represent, and on which his national populist narrative relies.

We would also suggest that, in the real world, the graduate class – though undeniably leaning left on social issues – is *increasingly* unlikely to support the interests of global finance capital.

Over the last half century, the decline of traditional industrial employment has led to a vast growth of a 'salariat' in white-collar, office jobs in technical, administrative and supervisory roles, alongside a growing number of public service employees in education, health and social care. These are the social strata – often graduates – who Goodwin and the wider national populist punditry caricature as the Thatcher–Blairite New Elite.

Yet, in reality, the economic issues facing the salaried classes – falling real wages, insecure working conditions, higher housing and energy costs – are similar to those facing other workers. Why else have over 200,000 university staff, half a million teachers and a million nurses, doctors and health workers been engaged in strikes and industrial action?

At the same time Goodwin and other national populist ideologues ignore the *actual* power elite, the 1% of global movers and shakers, the media moguls, hedge fund managers and directors of the new internet-based commercial giants. Nor do national populist ideologues address the huge influence and clout wielded by billionaire press owners and their role in promoting populist politics, whether Silvio Berlusconi in Italy, Vincent Bolloré in France or Rupert Murdoch in the UK and US. Doubtless some global capitalists are liberal on social issues. But the vast majority of people who believe in women's and LGBT+ rights, anti-racism and the need to combat climate change do not own hedge funds or head to Davos by private jet every winter.

On the basis of the nearly 13m (12,878,460) people who voted for a socially liberal, economically inter-ventionist Labour manifesto in the 2017 election, they are also likely to support greater equality, a more generous welfare state and an active role for governments in the economy.

Hence the fact that 87% of 'elitist', anti-equality Remainers think income gaps in Britain are too wide, ten points ahead of the 77% of populist, egalitarian Leavers who think the same thing.[159] Most striking of all are the significant majorities among both groups in favour of greater equality.

Having miscategorised the 'bad guys' in the New Elite, national populists also misrepresent the 'good guys' in the general population, imposing on them views they increasingly don't hold. Having created a fantasy minority, they've had to create a fantasy majority to match.

THE MYTH OF THE CONSERVATIVE MAJORITY

National populism relies on the idea of a homogenous white working class with socially traditional opinions, increasingly shifting to the conservative right. It's true that both Britain's Conservatives and America's Republicans consolidated support among sections of working-class voters (particularly in smaller towns and the countryside) and so became more cross-class coalitions. But, as we've seen, most Brexit voters were southern Conservatives and Trump comfortably beat Biden among the better off.

The mythology of a new conservative working-class vote goes deeper. After the Brexit vote, much attention was paid to Lord Ashcroft's immense (12,369) exit poll and its analysis of social attitudes among voters in the referendum.[160] Ashcroft chose a series of contemporary sociopolitical phenomena (including multiculturalism, social liberalism, feminism, the green movement, globalism, capitalism and immigration) and asked his sample whether they saw them as forces for good or ill.

If you take approval or disapproval of these phenomena as an index of being socially liberal (force for good) or conservative (force for ill), then liberal people tended to vote Remain and illiberal people overwhelmingly voted Leave.

The report was however widely misunderstood and misrepresented. For example, while 81% of anti-multiculturalists voted Leave, only 47% of Leavers *as a whole* were anti-multiculturalist. Similarly, while 74% of voters who didn't like social liberalism voted Leave, only 38% of Leavers were opposed to social liberalism.

Overall, among both Leavers and Remainers, multiculturalism was seen as a force for ill by only 30% of the sample, social liberalism by 24%, the green movement by 20% and feminism by 16%.

The reason for this, of course, is that the British public is generally more liberal than illiberal. In the overall sample, immigration was the only topic which attracted more force-for-illers than force-for-gooders, and even then, not a majority (40% of the overall sample).

The fact is that, despite Brexit, the last 30 years have not seen a swing towards traditional values, but away from them. There has also been an extraordinary liberalisation in attitudes towards homosexuality, inter-racial marriage and extramarital sex. The latest British Social Attitudes survey[161] shows that the proportion of those believing that people who want children ought to get married fell from 70% in 1989 to 24% in 2022; 67% of people think that a sexual relationship between two people of the same sex is never wrong, compared with 17% in 1983; and support for abortion on the basis of a woman's decision has risen from 37% in 1983 to 76% now.

There has also been a marked decline in hostility to immigration post-Brexit, with 45% agreeing that there were too many immigrants in 2023, compared with 64% in 2013. Another survey showed the number saying immigration should be reduced declining from 65% to 42% between 2015 and 2022.[162] Hostility to transgender people and to immigration has seen a small uptick in the last two years, which may well be explained by the success of culture warriors in exciting alarm on those questions.

Perhaps the most eloquent poll is one conducted by YouGov in 2021,[163] which explored social attitudes in 52 constituencies across the North, the Midlands and Wales which went Conservative in 2019 (in other words, the 'red wall'). This found only marginal differences between supposedly anti-woke, socially conservative red wallers and the general population, and those very "luxury beliefs" which Goodwin insists divide the popular majority from the elite.

So 73% of the red wallers thought it was important to teach colonial history and the slave trade, as against 78% of the general population; half of red wallers thought the culture of people of different ethnic backgrounds was part of British culture (54% overall);

and 66% that climate change wasn't exaggerated, just one percent lower than the general population. The only substantial gap was on immigration, with those thinking it was a good thing (at 40%) a full 10% lower than the national average.

It's perhaps worth comparing that with a 2019 survey of Conservative Party members,[164] which found that 58% want to bring back hanging, 46% think climate change is exaggerated, 56% that Islam is a threat to the British way of life and 54% that Donald Trump would make a good prime minister. And a 2024 Opinium poll – also of Conservative Party members – found that only 35% had a positive view of LGBT+ people, and well under 30% felt positively about feminists, immigrants or Muslims. The number believing that Islam is a threat had risen to 58%, with 52% believing that parts of European cities are under sharia law and are no-go areas for non-Muslims.[165] So who is out of touch?

On the basis of these figures, it's no surprise that there has been a progressive majority – more people voting for Labour, Liberal Democrats, Greens, SNP and Plaid Cymru than for the Conservatives plus pro-Brexit parties – in every election this century except 2015. Even in the election of 2019, 14.6m people voted for the Conservative and Brexit parties and 16.2m for progressives.

WHERE IT CAN LEAD

Like any belief based on the denial of reality, the national populist conspiracy theory can lead on to even more dangerous beliefs. In the diatribes and polemics of its promoters there are distinct echoes of the deadly theory which led to the genocidal horrors of the Second World War.

The most toxic and influential conspiracy theory of the 20th century began in Russia with the publication in 1903 of a Tsarist secret police forgery *The Protocols of the Learned Elders of Zion*, purporting to outline the plan of a secret cabal of Jewish financiers to destroy the nation states and establish a one-world tyranny under their control. Among the weapons used to achieve this aim was the establishment of international institutions, the demoralising of populations by "cultural pollution" and the corruption of youth, ownership of the press, the encouragement of racial mixing and allying with Marxist revolutionaries:

"Nowadays, with the destruction of the aristocracy, the people have fallen into the grips of merciless money-grinding scoundrels who have laid a pitiless and cruel yoke upon the necks of the workers. We appear on the scene as the alleged saviours of the worker from this oppression and we suggest that he should enter the ranks of our fighting forces – Socialists, Anarchists, Communists – to whom we always give support."[166]

Drawing on a millennium of anti-Jewish prejudice, promoted by industrialist Henry Ford and despite being exposed as a forgery in *The Times* in 1921, the *Protocols* were hugely influential on Hitler. They were quoted in *Mein Kampf*, the Nazi Party published 23 editions of the book, and it was widely taught in schools. Not for nothing was Norman Cohn's magisterial account of the *Protocols* and their influence titled *Warrant for Genocide*.[167]

The theory reappears throughout the 20th century, in a variety of forms. In early 1960s America, the far-right John Birch Society claimed that "both the US and Soviet governments are controlled by the same furtive conspiratorial cabal of internationalists, greedy bankers and corrupt politicians".[168] The first chair of the British National Front, A.K. Chesterton, wrote a conspiratorial tract called *The New Unhappy Lords*, one of whose chapters is headed 'Is the conspiracy Jewish?' (answer, in his case, 'yes').[169] As we've seen, Enoch Powell claimed that "conspirators sit in the seats of the mighty",[170] including civil servants faking immigration figures to deceive the public.[171]

In *National Populism*, Eatwell and Goodwin acknowledge that Viktor Orban's version of the theory – international financiers plotting to destroy nation states by flooding them with immigrants – is a version of "anti-Semitic conspiracy theory", which makes it all the more striking when they assert that the claims – particularly against the "Hungarian-Jewish financier

George Soros" – are "not entirely without credence".[172] Goodwin's version of the theory – corporations plus white liberals allying with migrants against the white working class – neither consists of nor implies that the conspirators are Jewish. Nor did Donald Trump's claim (in a speech in Florida in 2016) that "Hillary Clinton meets in secret with international banks to plot the destruction of US sovereignty, in order to enrich those global financial powers"[173] specify their race. But the tone is a clear echo. So, in the same Florida speech, Trump declared that "the establishment and their media enablers wield control over this nation"; while the *Protocols* insist that "Through the press, we have gained the power to influence while remaining ourselves in the shade".[174]

In a 2018 speech, Viktor Orban echoed both the conspiratorial tone and much of the content of the *Protocols*, again without identifying his target as Jewish: "We must fight against an opponent which is different from us. Their faces are not visible, but hidden from view; they do not fight directly, but by stealth; they are not honourable, but unprincipled; they are not national, but international; they do not believe in work, but speculate with money; they have no homeland, but feel that the whole world is theirs."[175]

The *Protocols* are sometimes still believed: they were cited in Hamas's founding statement,[176] they were quoted as fact by a Greek Golden Dawn MP in October 2012,[177] and Poland's Law and Justice party's former minister of defence thinks they're probably genuine.[178]

Over the last decade, versions of the theory – with or without specifically anti-Semitic overtones – have been pumped out by national populists across Europe and North America. It would be wrong to accuse promoters of one element of the theory of thereby buying into the theory in its entirety. You can think that the liberal elite is encouraging a lowering of the birth rate without thinking it's in alliance with global finance capital. But it's clear from history that a taste for one item on the conspiratorial menu frequently leads people to try another.

At a time when a range of conspiracy theories are being trumpeted not just in social media and right-wing media outlets but also by current, former[179] or aspirant national leaders, promoting seemingly freestanding parts of the repertoire can prove a gateway drug to the whole.[180]

PROMOTING TRUMP

On top of his 2016 statement about conspiratorial global elites, Donald Trump's 2023–4 campaign language has been increasingly reminiscent of inter-war Nazi rhetoric. In a Veterans Day speech in November 2023, Trump pledged to root out "the communists, Marxists, fascists, and the radical left thugs that live like vermin within the confines of our country".[181] At a December 2023 New Hampshire rally, he repeated an earlier statement that immigrants were "poisoning the blood" of America.[182] He described Biden's immigration policy as a "conspiracy to overthrow the United States", declared "I only want to be a dictator for one day" and predicted a bloodbath if he doesn't get elected.[183]

Despite this, British national populists increasingly fell in line behind Trump as the 2024 election approached. As far back as January 2022, Unherd berated "the liberal fantasy of the Capitol coup"[184] and, in December 2023, asked 'Why all this Trump hysteria?'.[185] In November 2023, Spiked praised Trump for being "the first president in half a century" to make Americans feel "that the end of the American Dream was unacceptable".[186] And Boris Johnson insisted that "a Trump presidency could be just what the world needs".[187]

But the most dramatic turnaround was Matthew Goodwin's. In his co-written *National Populism*, he argued that Trump was not a fascist but a national populist.[188] After the Capitol coup, he admitted that Trump was now "closer to the fascists than populists".[189] In the wake of Trump's January 2024 primary victory, Goodwin lauded him as the champion of a "national conservatism", set finally to overthrow the globalist establishment in the interests of the working class.[190] As if 6 January 2021 had never happened.

IS NATIONAL POPULISM FASCIST?

Donald Trump and his ism raise the question of whether national populism is fascist, or on the way to it.

Fascism has been defined in many different ways since World War Two,[191] but fascist parties clearly share a number of characteristics. They are hyper-nationalist, xenophobic movements which emerge after an economic crisis has thrown existing political structures and systems into question. Glorifying an idealised and exclusive vision of national cultural identity, fascism locates a threat from a visible enemy or enemies, bound together by a conspiracy theory which seeks to explain "community decline, humiliation, or victimhood"[192] as the result of the machinations of secretive, international finance. A strong, charismatic leader directs an increasingly paramilitary bid for power.

Often winning power through legitimate elections, fascists create a 'managed democracy' (the term describes Mussolini's Italy)[193] in which opposition parties are constrained and then dismantled, human rights undermined and intermediate institutions (judiciary, media, trade unions, even churches) incorporated. Elections are abolished, and armed militias integrated within a state ruled by one party and indeed one leader.

The speed, extent and character of fascism as a movement and in power is determined by circumstances. Is there a powerful left-wing movement seeking itself to win power? Are existing institutions "in a state of blockage, apparently insoluble to the existing authorities?" Are traditional elites "tempted to look for tougher helpers to stay in charge?"[194] And is there a candidate for leader?

Clearly, the national populism which has emerged in the wake of the 2008 crash overlaps with fascism (nationalism, xenophobia, idealised national culture, identified threat, anti-global conspiracy theory, charismatic leader) but thus far movements aspiring to power have not been militarised and have remained within the rules of electoral democracy. In power, the position is more complex. In Europe, Viktor Orban certainly shares all the above elements, and he has also sought both to gerrymander the Hungarian electoral system and to undermine or incorporate the judiciary and the media. There are paramilitary vigilantes in Hungary attacking refugees and Roma[195] but they are not run by Orban's party. As elsewhere in Eastern Europe, Hungarian national populism faces alternative parties, in the case of Jobbik, with a paramilitary history, to Orban's right.

In America, Donald Trump shares all the overlapping characteristics with Viktor Orban. In addition, he encouraged an insurrection (in the case of the Proud Boys, in an organised, quasi-paramilitary group) intended to overthrow the result of the 2020 election. As we've seen, his language increasingly echoes pre-war German rhetoric – "vermin", "poisoning the blood" – and his rhetoric grows ever more threatening, promising "judgement day" and "ultimate and absolute revenge" against his political opponents, in a country where "the only thing standing between you and its obliteration is me".[196]

Largely accepting the constraints of the existing political system, eschewing paramilitary organisation and political violence, national populism is distinct from fascism and often serves as an alternative to it. But, as we've seen with conspiracy theories, it can also prove a gateway, as is the increasing danger with Trump and his supporters.

As stated in the introduction, we don't think national populism is fascist. But the danger of national populism proving not a barrier but a doorway to the further right is the first of many threats it poses to liberal democracy. The others are described in the next chapter.

CHAPTER 6

WHY DOES IT MATTER? COMBATTING THE CULTURAL DIVIDE

The rise of national populism across the world over the last two decades has been moulded by powerful and wealthy forces on the right of politics. They have reached out to the self-employed, the working classes and poorer sections of society, left exposed and vulnerable by the economic and social effects of the tech revolution and broader global change.

These new cross-class coalitions led from the right, often with a charismatic figurehead – think Trump, Bolsonaro, Johnson, Orban, Meloni – have received vocal backing from much of the billionaire press – in the UK from Murdoch (*Sun*, *Times*), Rothermere (*Daily Mail*), the Barclay brothers (*Telegraph*) – plus privately funded TV channels like GB News and new social media which largely skew to the populist right.

The impact of national populists and their media supporters has been immense: they have not only encouraged voting for national populist parties and policies, but have tried to pull the political centre of gravity rightwards.

BROKEN PROMISES:
DISAPPOINTING THE CONVERTS

National populism's key strategy is to appeal to its target constituencies on both culture and economics. In the US, Trump promised to end deindustrialisation and bring jobs and prosperity back to the industrial rustbelt. In Hungary, Viktor Orban's Fidesz implemented economically interventionist policies like raising the minimum wage, introducing a house-building programme and abolishing university tuition fees. In the UK's Brexit referendum campaign, the Leave campaign repeatedly asserted that leaving the EU would free up £350 million a week for the National Health Service. In 2019, Johnson's Conservatives successfully mobilised the Brexit vote in Labour areas by promising to build 40 new hospitals by 2030, and a 'levelling-up' programme to tackle the deindustrialisation and deprivation of the Midlands and North.

This realignment was celebrated by advocates of the new faultline like the *New Statesman* and praised in its pages by conservative columnist Simon Heffer, who claimed that "the political shift was made because of a conviction among working-class people that the Labour Party no longer understood their lives or ideals".[197] In fact, as we have shown, despite some shifts, the reality was that most Conservative and Trump voters in 2019 and 2020 were traditional conservative supporters.

The economic promises made by national populist politicians have proved to be empty rhetoric once populists are in office. Under Trump the promises to rebuild the nation's infrastructure simply didn't materialise: all Trump managed was building some of his border wall. His major economic legacy was a spectacular tax cut for the rich.

In Hungary, secure in his 2010 supermajority, Orban imposed a flat-rate tax of 16%, amended the Labour Code to weaken employee and trade union rights, significantly raised the overtime hours which employees could be required to work and reduced the job-seeker benefit from nine months to three.[198] Having abolished university student fees, Fidesz initiated a referendum which reinstated them.

In the UK, the 2019 Conservatives' manifesto promise to build 40 new hospitals was soon downgraded, with the figure revealed to include building new wings or refurbishment of existing hospitals.[199] Meanwhile, waiting lists for hospital treatment grew to record levels. On levelling-up: the previous EU funds to renovate designated areas and retrain the labour force came to an end. Instead of guaranteed subsidies over seven years, the Conservatives introduced seven short-term programmes, adding up to a fraction of previous grants from the EU.[200] In the first year, less than 3% of the Levelling-Up Fund was delivered, and, in the year to March 2022, the South-East received £9.2m as against the North-East's £4.9m.[201]

When talking to Conservative party activists, Rishi Sunak boasted that, as chancellor, he'd taken public money out of "deprived urban areas" to help wealthier towns:[202] "I managed to start changing the funding formulas to make sure areas like this are getting the funding they deserved."[203] The area was wealthy Tunbridge Wells.

As 2019 manifesto policy chief Rachel Wolf admitted a year later, the Conservative government had a choice, either to focus on the "just about managing" or on "affluent Britain" but could not do both. They chose the latter.[204] Elected on a national populist economic programme, the Conservatives didn't want to find the resources necessary to tackle deindustrialisation and address the needs of the "just about managing".

Instead, national populist politicians and commentators downgrade economic issues and mobilise their supporters around issues of culture, tradition, nationhood and identity. Indeed, against the evidence of opinion polls,[205] John Gray argues that "early 21st century political conflict is more value based than it is economic in origin".[206]

ROLLING BACK GAINS ON GENDER, SEXUALITY AND RACE

In Hungary, Orban's Fidesz stresses women's role as mothers and child-bearers, with the government offering extended tax breaks for those rearing more children; similar pro-natalist, socially conservative preoccupations are a key feature of the New Conservative group in the UK led by MPs Miriam Cates, an evangelical Christian, and Danny Kruger, ex-prime minister Johnson's political secretary. In Spain, Vox's rise has been associated with vociferous anti-feminist campaigning; in Poland, PIS outlawed LGBT+ rights and passed legislation effectively outlawing abortion; while in the US the Republican-dominated Supreme Court, secured during the Trump presidency, overturned the 1973 Roe vs Wade judgment in June 2022, criminalising abortion in many states.

Yet the most common, indeed ubiquitous, element that unites national populists is its hostility to newcomers, migrants and refugees. This was central to Trump's presidential campaign in 2016; to the success of the Leave campaign in the Brexit referendum; to the rise of populist parties across Scandinavia; to Orban's continued success in Hungary; and to Geert Wilders' victory in the November 2023 Dutch election.

The post-war *cordon sanitaire* kept the racist, nationalist right at bay. Now it is in tatters, and traditional conservatives have increasingly joined the racist, anti-migrant chorus.

PULLING POLITICS EVER RIGHTWARD

The UK has proved no exception. Ever since Boris Johnson's purge of one-nation Conservatives from the parliamentary party, the Conservative government has been dominated by various shades of the hard right. Whipped up by the Brexit press, the venom directed at migrants, most especially refugees and asylum seekers, has escalated. In October 2022, then home secretary Suella Braverman declared in the House of Commons: "Let us be clear about what is really going on here: the British people deserve to know which party is serious about stopping the invasion on our southern coast."[207] It was the first time a minister had used the military language of invasion. She continued in similar vein six months later when introducing the Illegal Migration Bill: "There are 100 million people around the world who could qualify for protection under our current laws. Let us be clear. They are coming here."[208]

It could have been 120 years earlier, when the *Daily Mail* ran a regular series of news stories and opinion features under the strapline 'The Alien Invasion', as it condemned the influx of Jews fleeing from pogroms in Tsarist Russia and Eastern Europe. The common features between then and today are striking: the key role of the right-wing press; the scare stories on numbers; the assertion that the new migrants would never be able to integrate; and the repeated efforts to mobilise cross-class alliances behind the anti-migrant cause.[209]

Then as now, the migration question drove politicians to conjure up outlandish ideas. The proposal to deport people fleeing from war and persecution to Rwanda – 4,000 miles from Britain – is not the first time that Conservative politicians have dreamt up a policy of shipping unwanted newcomers off to distant lands. As colonial secretary 120 years ago, Joseph Chamberlain thought the deserted hilltop terrain of the Mau Escarpment in East Africa would be an ideal site for the resettlement of Jews fleeing persecution in Europe. Called the 'Uganda Scheme', it gave him the chance both to play the humanitarian hero – a statesman making a practical offer to a beleaguered people – and to promote a strong nativist policy to his working-class base.

When he went to speak to the working classes in East London in 1904, the *Daily Mail* reported that he was greeted with great enthusiasm: "Limehouse and its neighbours do not love the aliens and welcomed Mr Chamberlain's idea of establishing them in the unoccupied space of East Africa." The plan found less enthusiasm among Jews and was quietly dropped.[210]

During the Brexit campaign, Michael Gove and the Vote Leave camp[211] claimed that, following Turkey's entry into the EU (unlikely then, improbable now), 76 million people could flood into the country. The tone and language of government ministers echoes that of the billionaire Conservative press and is designed to demonise refugees and promote division and hatred.

It chimes with right-wing politicians in other parts of Europe, whose rhetoric is also pulling mainstream parties to the right. In 2016, Austria's social democrat chancellor Werner Faymann reversed a decision to back Angela Merkel's opening of German borders to Syrian refugees, sided with the centre-right People's Party in closing Austria's border and persuaded other states to do the same.[212] In 2017, Geert Wilders' claim that "Moroccan scum" were making the Dutch streets unsafe provoked mainstream conservative prime minister Mark Rutte to write an open letter, calling on foreigners who "abuse our freedom" to leave.[213] In 2021, Denmark's social democratic prime minister Mette Frederiksen announced her ambition for Denmark not to offer asylum to any refugees at all.[214]

In 2023, France's President Macron's government passed an anti-immigration law which reduced migrants' access to welfare, toughened rules for foreign students, introduced migration quotas and made it harder for the children of non-nationals to become French; Marine le Pen described the bill as an "ideological victory".[215] And following his 2023 victory over the far-right Law and Justice Party in Poland, centrist Donald Tusk declared in February 2024 that combating mass/illegal immigration was nothing less than "a question of the survival of our Western civilisation", a speech greeted with predictable glee by Unherd.[216]

THE THREAT TO DEMOCRACY

Everywhere national populists are fighting a multi-targeted culture war with a single objective: to divide and split the old alliance of the working and professional classes which brought about so much progressive reform last century. The strategy is wrapped in the embrace of an idealised nation state, on which rock lodges a supposedly unchanging culture, identity and tradition. As Douglas Murray so inappropriately put it at the National Conservatism Conference, even if the Germans had "mucked up" twice in the 20th century, nationalism is the future and Brexit – having freed the UK from the shackles of Europe – is the opportunity.[217]

Since populists claim that in their battle against elites they alone represent the 'will of the people', in power they usually seek to erode the checks and balances of a liberal democratic system. So, national populists attack the democratic processes which brought them to office. They have undermined the independence of the judiciary in Poland, Hungary and the United States; they appointed political loyalists to control the state media in Poland and Hungary; their control of that media has meant that the governing parties gain disproportionate airtime during elections. With government connivance, vigilantes patrol border fences in Hungary, Bulgaria and the United States, while in the US, Republicans have both attempted to gerrymander the electoral roll in many states and then in 2020 attempted to rig the election results by getting sympathetic officials to increase Republican tallies and discount Democratic ones.[218] Trump has promised his followers "I am your retribution", threatening to use presidential powers to pardon the 6 January 2021 rioters, to prosecute enemies and to use the Insurrection Act to crush domestic protest.[219]

In addition to attacks on democratic procedures by self-proclaimed democrats like Orban and Trump, anti-democratic opinions and advocates are becoming increasingly popular, particularly among the young. A worldwide 2023 survey found that only 57% of 18–35-year-olds were supportive of democracy, and 35% felt a strong leader who didn't hold elections or consult parliament was "a good way to run a country".[220] A 2019 Hansard audit found that more than half of British voters favoured rule by "a strong leader willing to break the rules".[221] In October 2023, PayPal and Palantir founder Peter Thiel, who announced in 2009 that he "no longer believe[s] that freedom and democracy are compatible",[222] was introduced and interviewed by John Gray while delivering – yes – The Roger Scruton Memorial Lecture, titled 'The Diversity Myth', at Oxford University.

The populist danger is real. Across Europe and America, in India and Latin America, the New Elite narrative is being promoted by the shock troops of the culture wars, risking the social and cultural gains of past decades. As we have shown, conspiracy theories with terrifying antecedents are taking hold. Almost half (47%) of leave voters believed the government deliberately concealed the truth about how many immigrants live in the UK, while 31% of Leave voters believed that Muslim immigration was part of a wider plot to make Muslims the majority in Britain.[223]

As we saw in Chapter 5, a majority of Conservative Party members believe that Islam is a threat and that parts of cities are no-go areas. Such beliefs have percolated upwards through the party. In February 2024, former home secretary Suella Braverman claimed that "the Islamists, the extremists and the antisemites are in charge now".[224] Later the same month former deputy chair of the Conservative Party, Lee Anderson, declared that, while he didn't believe that "Islamists have got control of our country", he did believe "they've got control of [Mayor Sadiq] Khan, and they've got control of London".[225] Conspiratorialist and authoritarian ideas are spreading from national populist ideologues via leading figures in mainstream parties into the wider population.

Progressives must recognise the danger and fight back, rebuilding the pluralist coalition that did so much good in the past. The next chapter suggests how this can be done.

CHAPTER 7

THE PROGRESSIVE ALTERNATIVE

We live in dangerous and disorienting times. The growing menace of the illiberal, anti-democratic right presents real dangers, in many ways reminiscent of the 1930s. One urgent task is to expose the fallacies, fantasies and flaws of national populism, which we have detailed in this book.

But there are political lessons to be learnt from the disaster of the 1930s in Europe. Now, as then, this threat can be defeated. The standout lesson is clear: unite against the main enemy; develop broad campaigns that mobilise a wide alliance of social forces; and offer an optimistic vision for the future. After all, the UK and most of Europe are very wealthy, if unequal, countries.

In this chapter, we outline what we think is the current political configuration, and how progressives can address the concerns which national populists exploit, with realistic alternative policies, from the economy and climate change to immigration. We look at ways of challenging political, ethnic and geographical divides, and, first, what tactical dangers to shun.

CUL-DE-SACS TO AVOID

In developing this popular alternative there are four cul-de-sacs that progressives need to avoid.

First, and most importantly, social democracy and the wider progressive movement has to shed its attachment to the neoliberal, Third Way model of globalisation if it is to repair its lost links with working-class and low-income households. National populists won't be defeated by offering reheated versions of globalisation and the monetarist orthodoxy responsible for the financial crash, wage stagnation and rising inequalities that have caused the current crisis.

Second, parts of the left echo the national populist right and still hanker for an alternative strategy based on national boundaries.[226] In today's world this is impossible. The relatively small and medium-sized nations of Europe all rely on production processes and integrated supply chains that operate across borders. Around 3.1 million lorry journeys were made from the UK to Europe in the year to June 2023.[227] The pattern is the same across the continent. For all European nations the optimal economic area is continental in scale.

The progressive alternative to hyperglobalisation cannot be a retreat to nationalist boltholes, as Jean-Luc Mélenchon's left-wing La France Insoumise party proposes. Instead, it must develop a trans-European strategy which corresponds to the realities of the 21st-century economy and the profound challenges thrown up by the environmental crisis. It has to articulate alternative models of economic and social life that reflect these realities and show how countries can collaborate across borders.

Thirdly, there are nativists on the left who ape the hard right on migration. As we have seen, the Danish Social Democrats explicitly copied the harsh immigration and refugee policies of the populist Danish People's Party and introduced them in government. This opportunist move cuts across basic social democratic principles of equality and solidarity and makes it harder for social democrats to promote principled policies elsewhere in an increasingly multi-ethnic Europe. In Britain, Maurice Glasman abandoned his 2011 call for an immigration ban, but Blue Labour advocate Jonathan Rutherford insists that Labour "must have the courage to reduce immigration", citing "national identity, community cohesion and cultural difference" as among the reasons.[228] We are not in favour of open borders, but nor do we favour a polarising, culturally based anti-immigration policy which divides people and defines citizenship on ethnic and racial grounds.

Fourthly, when the hard right are busy stirring up cultural wars, progressives need to combat sectarian ideas which unwittingly help them. Within the anti-racist movement some propose a narrow identity politics where only direct, personal experience counts. Yet millions across the world didn't need to be black South Africans to campaign against apartheid. Defending the rights of women, people of colour and the LGBT+ community should not lead progressives down the dead-end of divisive identity politics and cancel culture, which denies empathy and solidarity.

THE CHANGING TIDE

Side-stepping these pitfalls, a progressive coalition can build an uplifting programme that addresses the big issues of our time. In three key areas in the battle against national populism – the economy, migration and culture wars – there are signs that the tide is moving in a progressive direction. But to capitalise on this potential, progressives have to shed the defensiveness that has characterised them in recent years.

On the economy the zeitgeist is changing, and one half of the hitherto prevalent orthodoxy is being discarded. Until the climate emergency and COVID, most European social democrats stayed wedded to the neoliberal tenets of the Maastricht Treaty and the Stability and Growth Pact. As the failings of neoliberalism have become starker, the centre of gravity in economic debate has moved left, with the need for large-scale state intervention increasingly accepted. The EU led the way with its unprecedented €750 billion green recovery programme 'Repair and Prepare for the Next Generation'.[229] The International Monetary Fund (IMF) and the Organisation for Economic Co-Operation and Development (OECD) reversed four decades of Washington consensus and gave their seal of approval to public investment strategies. With its Inflation Reduction Act,[230] the Biden administration has demonstrated that interventionist, industrial strategies and active government can be brought back.

Labour's stance is contradictory. On the one hand, shadow chancellor Rachel Reeves has followed suit, in May 2023 boldly announcing her "new business model for Britain".[231] An interventionist industrial strategy centred on the transition to a low-carbon economy, this offered a distinct break from New Labour. But while one wing of stifling neoliberal doctrine has collapsed, Labour remains tied to fiscal orthodoxy (monetarism). Like UK chancellor Jeremy Hunt's calls for balanced budgets, Germany's finance minister, Christian Lindner, argues for the retention of the EU's regressive Stability and Growth Pact which, ironically, cramps growth. At the same time, like many within the broader liberal and green left, Labour baulks at calling for a new social settlement that would tackle the gross inequalities, wealth disparities and high-carbon excesses that have escalated across the West. Here, Reeves and Keir Starmer have displayed a stultifying caution,[232] pandering to the financial orthodoxies of the neoliberal era, exemplified by the scaling back of their Green Deal programme in February 2024. This unresolved tension was very evident in Reeves' widely reported Mais lecture to City leaders in March 2024.[233]

Yet there is increasing, heavyweight backing for serious interventionist strategies. The French economist Thomas Piketty has laid out a general framework for what could be done.[234] The UK and its European neighbours remain rich countries where revenue could be raised to put public services back on a proper footing, lift the social safety net and pay for green housing renovation and job support programmes.

In December 2023, a report from the Resolution Foundation, 'Ending Stagnation: A New Economic Strategy for Britain' showed that Britain is suffering from a poisonous combination of stalled productivity and high inequality.[235] This combination means that "typical households are 9% poorer than their French counterparts while our low-income families are 27% poorer".[236] Key recommendations included prioritising public investment, which is nearly 50% higher in other OECD countries; taxing wealth, which has risen from three times national income in the 1980s to seven times in 2023; reconnecting benefit levels with wages; and focusing on Britain being a "services superpower" (it's already the world's second biggest exporter of services after the US).[237] Here is the terrain on which to recreate a new progressive coalition, restore the public realm and expose the empty claims of national populists that they are on the side of the working class.

On migration and refugees the task is harder. But rather than mimic the populists, progressives need to set out their own stall. On refugees, the right to offer shelter to those fleeing war and persecution set out in the 1951 Geneva Convention remains as valid as ever. Furthermore, this should be a responsibility shared by countries across Europe rather than borne exclusively by Mediterranean countries. Claims should be processed quickly in the host country and asylum seekers allowed to work while awaiting a decision, thereby making a net contribution to the country.

On migration, progressives need to challenge the national populist mindset. Since the Second World War, Western European economies have required immigrant labour. With an ageing population and declining birth rates that trend will continue. There are push factors like climate change and swift population growth encouraging migration from Africa to Europe but the key pull factor remains the demand for labour across the global North.

Look at Italy. In opposition, Giorgia Meloni lambasted the "dark forces" of migration. But within a year of taking office she has discreetly changed her tune. In summer 2023 Meloni's legal migration decrees specifically agreed to 452,000 migrant workers from 2023 to 2025 to fill seasonal jobs in sectors like agriculture and tourism as well as long-term positions like plumbers, electricians, mechanics and care workers.[238] It's a similar story in Greece.[239] While the UK net annual migration figure up to June 2023 of 672,000 was exceptional, it's quite clear that demand for labour means that inward migration must continue for the foreseeable future to ensure critical roles such as those in the NHS and social care are filled.

Increasing numbers of the public recognise that once migrants settle they contribute to the country's prosperity. This book's authors both live in Birmingham. Here, mixed workplaces are the norm: in factories and offices, hi-tech science parks and hospitals. Second- and third-generation migrants are increasingly present in business, public services and the professions. At Aston and Birmingham City universities, around 50% of the students come from ethnic minority backgrounds; 19.7% of households in the city with two or more people living in them are mixed race.[240]

Migrants have put down roots, see Birmingham as their home and have an affection and affinity with the city. Their integration has been a positive story. Whatever Nigel Farage might wish, there is no going back to the mono-cultural world of the 1950s.

At a macro-level the issue is how governments can manage future migration flows to match economic needs and cooperate with other countries where necessary. At a micro-level the issue is how to make these multi-ethnic towns and cities – from Birmingham to Berlin and Barcelona – work better. Tensions remain, worsened by two decades of wage stagnation and substantial cuts to public services. Multiculturalism can lapse into plural monoculturalism,[241] where some wish to retain a separate, 'fenced-off' identity, with different ethnic communities living side by side but with little, if any, interaction. This allows religious fundamentalists to use issues such as sex education in schools to whip up controversy and promote an agenda of separate development.

Progress on combating these challenges is varied but it is real. The traditionalists and nativists don't like it, but a new, mixed country is emerging and increasingly accepted.[242]

On culture wars, the changing mood was evident during the 2021 Euro football tournament.[243] The global impact of the Black Lives Matter movement was followed by footballers and athletes showing their solidarity by 'taking the knee'. This produced a veritable explosion of bile and hatred from the national populist right. With the England football team at the Euros declaring its intention to show its opposition to racism in sport and wider society, the hard right thought they had a juicy target. Before the tournament, home secretary Priti Patel decried the move as "gesture politics". Through his press spokesperson, prime minister Boris Johnson refused to condemn those booing the team.

Yet, in the aftermath of the competition, it was clear that the strategy had backfired. More fans chose to cheer and applaud the team when it took the knee at kick-off; many opposing teams showed solidarity by following suit; the multiracial squad exceeded expectations; and when the team lost on penalties in the final, and racist abuse of three players followed, there was an outcry with overwhelming support for them. Suddenly, Conservative politicians were falling over themselves to praise the team and decry the racists. This is yet more evidence that national populists' stances on these issues are not principled but opportunistic.

When the home secretary condemned the racist abuse, England player Tyrone Mings responded: "You don't get to stoke the fire at the beginning of the tournament by labelling our anti-racism message as 'Gesture Politics' and then pretend to be disgusted when the very thing we're campaigning against, happens."[244]

For progressives, Euro 2021 showed three ways to tackle cultural clashes: the importance of focusing on the core issue; the role of leadership, as England manager Gareth Southgate demonstrated by setting the terms of the debate; and the need to rebut hard. As a result, Patel, Johnson and the government got their fingers burnt.

It was similar after the Women's World Cup in 2023 when the huge wave of support across Europe and beyond for the victorious Spanish team showed that sexist values have declining purchase among the general population.

We have shown how, in addition to anti-racism, support for progressive social causes like feminism and LGBT+ rights is increasing. It's worth remembering how the 2022 US midterm elections demonstrated that defending the social gains of the last half-century is not just morally right but an election winner. A total of 76% of Democrats rated abortion as an important or very important issue in the midterms, in which the party did unexpectedly well, particularly where they focused on the topic.[245]

PROMOTING A WIDER PROGRESSIVE AGENDA

This approach to tackling the populist right can be adopted elsewhere. Below we look at four key areas.

First, climate change. Summer 2023 confirmed for all but the delusional the alarming reality of the pace of climate change. Heatwaves, forest fires and mass floods scarred the northern hemisphere. There were welcome, if belated, signs that the major powers are beginning to respond. The latest report on renewables from the authoritative International Energy Agency shows that renewable capacity – primarily wind and solar – is expanding exponentially across the globe. It is expected to become the largest source of global electricity generation by early 2025, surpassing coal. Its share of the power mix is forecast to increase by 10% in the five-year period 2022–2027, reaching 38% by 2027.[246]

National populism is unable to respond to the challenge. Some politicians, like Lord Frost, remain in denial;[247] John Gray derides the green movement and claims it is too late to stop climate change;[248] the Sunak government reneged on its net zero commitments. Yet a progressive agenda is not difficult to chart: promote on-shore wind farms – now the *cheapest form* of energy; make renewable energy obligatory on all new housing and commercial developments; and facilitate the speedy expansion of solar. The shift to electric vehicles is accelerating quickly too, with global sales increasing by 55% in 2022.[249]

The insulation of buildings and the shift from gas boilers to electrical heating will be the biggest challenge. The UK has the oldest and draughtiest housing stock in Europe. Labour's Warmer Homes programme took the greatest hit when the worsening financial outlook and the fiscally conservative sections of Labour's leadership led Keir Starmer to announce a retreat from Labour's £28 billion per year green plan in February 2024.[250]

Yet the challenge won't disappear; rapid decarbonisation of housing stock remains central to the country meeting its climate change policy commitments. All serious proponents of the policy argue for a socially just transition with its costs borne by those most able to bear them. It is why an environmentalist government needs to offer generous and extensive grants for all households, as occurs in Germany[251] and France,[252] so that a wholesale programme of house renovation can be undertaken, improving homes and creating jobs. It's a programme that would also contribute enormously to a serious levelling-up agenda.

HEALING GEOGRAPHIC DIVIDES: A COVENANT FOR TOWNS

One of the most pernicious strands of national populist thinking divides 'bohemian' metropolitan cities from the 'common-sense' inhabitants of older industrial towns; in David Goodhart's parlance, setting cosmopolitan university-trained 'anywheres' against the rooted 'somewheres'.

The progressive response should promote urban development agendas that address the structural failings of the neoliberal era, particularly in former industrial heartlands. The reality is that growth is geographically uneven, with the higher-skilled jobs concentrated in larger metropolitan cities with more extensive IT, universities and better transport connections. Across Europe, big cities have been growing, sucking in young talent from neighbouring towns and the countryside.

Only government intervention can check these trends and inaugurate a genuine 'levelling-up' agenda. A 'Covenant for Towns' could lay out a set of facilities, capacities and policies which any town in 21st-century Britain should expect. Inspired by the concept of the proximity city, the goal would be for all citizens to be in easy walking or cycling distance – or a short bus ride – from a doctor's surgery, dentist, library, park, food and clothing stores, newsagent and café.

Within each town, core institutions would include a vocational college, with its sporting, cultural, educational and library facilities open to the general population and a hospital with an A&E department. Devolved planning powers would encourage new start-ups of industrial and retail companies encouraged by rent subsidies and council tax discounts, supporting young artisans and entrepreneurs who might otherwise leave. Mayor Andy Burnham's recent promotion of technical education for the industrial towns of the Greater Manchester city region is one example of what could be done.[253]

There are also lessons to be learnt from the cities. In power locally, Labour transformed many post-industrial cities through imaginative strategies of culture-led development in the 1980s and 1990s. Cities of Culture like Liverpool, Hull and now Bradford are doing the same.

CONFRONTING THE BREXIT HOT POTATO

Brexit remains at the heart of the national populist story. Matthew Goodwin still claims that "Brexit ushered us all into an incredibly exciting and entirely new era in our national history".[254] Yet, quite quickly and with no political prompting, the general public has seen through the moonshine. They have realised there are few, if any, "Brexit opportunities".[255]

Any campaign to re-join the EU now is a complete non-starter. But that should not mean that public policy should be frozen by the recent past. For reasons of economics, geography, history, culture and security, a close working partnership between the UK and the Continent is in the interests of both parties. In the 21st century, no country – whatever its history – can ever walk alone. Progressives can challenge the untenable premises of a hard Brexit and change the terms of the UK's political debate on Europe. How?

Firstly, on the economy progressive parties should state unequivocally that they have no intention of de-aligning from the regulatory framework of the single market. There will be no race to the bottom on industrial, environmental or social standards. This will create the conditions where a new government can discuss revising the Trade and Cooperation Agreement (TCA) so that a new economic partnership with the EU can be explored that would benefit both parties.[256]

Secondly, Ukraine has shown the need to add a defence component to the TCA. NATO is an alliance for military operations. Yet today both the UK and EU countries need ongoing cooperation on defence, weapons procurement and security issues and that can most effectively happen in close partnership with the EU.

Thirdly, on a range of research, educational and social issues – the Horizon programme, Erasmus/Leonardo exchanges, travel rules – a progressive UK government would need to repair the Brexit damage.

The government should be confident that there is a growing electoral majority that shuns the nationalist hype of the Farageists and wants the UK to develop cooperative relations with our European neighbours.

A REAL AND REALISTIC PLURALISM

Politically, the programme we advocate can only succeed if undertaken in a spirit of pluralism and openness. Today's more diverse, less deferential society makes grass-roots mobilisation and civic pluralism essential. A popular mobilisation of a diverse range of forces and parties will be crucial to create the progressive wave necessary to sweep away the corrosive fear generated by the populist right. This is even truer in Europe where proportional electoral systems predominate. The 2023 elections in Spain and Poland show that where all parts of the progressive spectrum work together, the forward march of national populism can be halted.

The hyperglobalist dreams of the 1990 neoliberals are fading fast, and being replaced by the nationalist right. Democracy is under threat not just from outright autocrats, but by 'strong leaders' like Orban,

Erdogan, Putin and Trump who, once elected, dismantle the checks and balances which preserve open debate, the rights of minorities and the conduct of free and fair elections.

Yet, despite all this, narrow nationalism and insularity go against the realities of our times. The 21st century is an age of ever-increasing international communication, where there exists more international trade and exchange than ever before, and where majorities want wealth more evenly shared. Our era is one of growing social diversity, with more and more people living in a country in which they or their parents were not born; where climate change increasingly reminds us that 'no man is an island'; and where access to greater birth control and education have rightly given more women than ever before unprecedented opportunities and freedom.

These are reasons why societies need to be open, outward looking and cooperative if they are going to shape the future. Progressives should be confident that their values chime with the age. This book has exposed many of the dangers of the populist right and the traps they set. But the conditions are there to offer and implement an uplifting programme of progressive, realistic change that fits our times. Are we up to the task?

ENDNOTES

1 'Fascist rally in Rome sparks Italian opposition outrage', Reuters, 8 January 2024.

2 GB News, 23 February 2024.

3 'German far-right met to plan "mass deportations"', BBC News, 11 January 2024; for original report see https://correctiv.org/en/top-stories/2024/01/15/secret-plan-against-germany.

4 Matthew Goodwin, 'The strange death of Labour Britain', Sunday Times, 2 June 2019.

5 Quoted in Jacques Rupnik, 'The crisis of liberalism', *Journal of Democracy* 29(3), July 2018.

6 John Gray, 'Progressives dream of tyranny', *New Statesman*, 10 November 2023.

7 Full text of Tony Blair's speech, BBC News, 27 September 2005.

8 UK Labour Market Statistics Research Briefing, House of Commons Library, 16 January 2024.

9 Rui Costa and Stephen Machin, 'Real wages and living standards in the UK', Centre for Economic Performance, LSE, May 2017.

10 Liz Fekete, *Europe's Fault Lines: Racism and the Rise of the Right*, Verso, 2017, p. 103.

11 See Kenan Malik, *Not So Black and White, A History of Race from White Supremacy to Identity Politics*, Hurst 2023, pp. 275–7.

12 Jan-Werner Muller, 'Poland after PiS', *London Review of Books*, 16 November 2023.

13 Zsuzsanna Szelenyi, *Tainted Democracy: Viktor Orban and the Subversion of Hungary*, Hurst, 2022, p. 77.

14 ibid, p84

15 Shaun Walker, 'Viktor Orban trumpets Hungary's "procreation, not immigration" policy', *The Guardian*, 6

September 2019.

16 Szelenyi, op. cit., pp. 276–7.

17 Ivan Krastev and Stephen Holmes, *The Light that Failed*, Penguin, 2019, p. 35.

18 Fekete, *Europe's Fault Lines*, p. 118.

19 Neal Ascherson, 'The assault on democracy in Poland is dangerous for the Poles and all Europe', *The Guardian*, 17 January 2016.

20 James Tilley, *The Kids are Alt Right?*, BBC Radio Four, 15-19 January, 2024

21 'Luis Montenegro appointed Portugal's prime minister' (in French), *Le Monde*, 21 March 2024.

22 Paul Foot, *The Rise of Enoch Powell*, Penguin, 1969, p. 129.

23 Enoch Powell speech at Birmingham Northfield, 13 June 1970.

24 Enoch Powell speech at Wolverhampton, 11 June 1970.

25 *Spearhead*, December 1976.

26 *Spearhead*, April 1971.

27 Andy Beckett, *When the Lights Went Out: What Really Happened to Britain in the Seventies*, Faber and Faber, 2009, p. 442.

28 Maurice Cowling (ed.), *Conservative Essays*, Cassell, 1978, p. 148.

29 Roger Scruton, *The Meaning of Conservatism*, Pelican, 1980, p. 16.

30 John Casey, 'One nation: the politics of race', *Salisbury Review*, Autumn 1982.

31 Editorial, *Salisbury Review*, Summer 1983.

32 Roger Scruton, 'Should he have spoken?', *New Criterion*, September 2006.

33 Robert Ford and Matthew Goodwin, *Revolt on the Right*, Routledge, p. 253.

34 Ibid., pp.. 146–7.

35 Brendan Carlin, 'Off-the-cuff Cameron accuses UKIP of being "fruitcakes and closet racists"', *Daily Telegraph*, 5 April 2006.

36 Aidan White, 'Migrant "cockroaches" and the need to tame tabloid hate', *Open Democracy*, 27 April 2015.

37 Nigel Farage, 'Who are you?', Channel 4, 31 March 2014.

38 Peter Walker, 'Nigel Farage basks in the triumph of his new dawn', *The Guardian*, 24 June 2016.

39 Jonathan Read, 'Boris Johnson refuses to apologise for "bum boys" and "letterboxes" remarks', *New European*, 22 November 2019.

40 Jim Pickard and Henry Mance, 'Theresa May: what she said and what it meant', *Financial Times*, 13 July 2016.

41 Theresa May, Conservative conference speech, 5 October 2016.

42 Danny Dorling, 'The geography and demography of Brexit', Mutiny Blog, 6 January 2020.

43 National Exit Polls: How Different Groups Voted, New York Times, 3 November 2020

44 Jonathan Freedland, 'Welcome to the age of Trump', *The Guardian*, 19 May 2016.

45 Chris Curtis (2017) 'How Britain voted at the 2017 General Election', YouGov, 13 June 2017.

46 Matthew Goodwin tweet, 27 June 2019.

47 Quoted in Douglas Murray, *Neoconservatism: Why We Need It*, Encounter, 2006, p. 89.

48 Sir Alfred Sherman Obituary, *The Times*, 29 August 2006.

49 Sir Alfred Sherman Obituary, *Daily Telegraph*, 28 August 2006.

50 Phillip Blond, 'Rise of the red Tories', *Prospect*, February 2009; also see Phillip Blond, *Red Tory: How Left and Right Have Broken Britain and How We Can Fix It*, Faber, 2010,

51 Rowena Davis, *Tangled up in Blue*, Ruskin Publishing, 2011, p. 2.

52 Dominic Sandbrook, 'Family, faith and flag', *New Statesman*, 7 April 2011.

53 Davis, op. cit., p. 176.

54 George Monbiot, 'Invasion of the entryists', *The Guardian*, 9 December 2003.

55 Jenny Turner, 'Who are they? Jenny Turner reports from the Battle of Ideas', *London Review of Books*, 8 July 2010.

56 Tim Montgomerie, 'The future of conservatism', *Prospect*, 15 July 2019.

57 Paul Embery, 'Woke is no substitute for political campaigning', Spiked, 20 December 2020.

58 Samuel Earle, 'Loud and uncowed: how UnHerd owner Paul Marshall became Britain's newest media mogul', The Guardian, 28 October 2023.

59 George Monbiot, 'How US billionaires are fuelling the hard-right cause in Britain', *The Guardian*, 7 December 2018.

60 Mick Hume, 'Only Boris Johnson can stop the Tories turning into a Blairite blancmange', *Daily Mail*, 21 October 2022.

61 Huw C. Davies and Sheena E. MacRae, 'An anatomy of the British war on woke', *Race & Class*, October–December 2023, pp. 15–16.

62 Ibid., p. 20.

63 Michael Shellenberger, 'Climate change is no catastrophe', Unherd, 3 November 2021.

64 Michael Schellenberger (interview), 'COP26 is a neo-feudal performance', Spiked, 8 November 2021.

65 Ibid.

66 Davis and MacRae, op. cit., p. 20.

67 Mary Harrington, 'The sexual revolution killed feminism', Unherd, 21 November 2021.

68 Ibid.

69 Ibid.

70 Mary Harrington, 'The feminist case against abortion', Spiked, 23 December 2021.

71 Paul Embery, 'Labour is still losing', Unherd, 21 January 2022.

72 Brendan O'Neill, 'Amber Heard and the crisis of feminism', Spiked, 28 May 2022.

73 Ella Whelan, 'International Women's Day is about everything but women', Spiked, 8 March 2022.

74 Kate Rosenfield, 'The white privilege of BLM, Unherd, May

17, 2022; Batya Ungar-Sargon, 'BLM supporters got what they paid for', Spiked, 20 May 2022.

75 https://www.gov.uk/government/publications/the-report-of-the-commission-on-race-and-ethnic-disparities

76 *Racism and Ethnic Inequality in a Time of Crisis*, Race Equality Foundation, 19 April 2023.

77 Police powers and procedures: Stop and search and arrests, England and Wales, year ending 31 March 2023.

78 Veena Raleigh, 'The health of people from ethnic minority groups in England', King's Fund, 17 May 2023.

79 Rakmid Ehsan, 'Tony Sewell is dead right about race', Spiked, 16 March 2022.

80 Mick Hume, 'Macpherson report: keeping our wits about us', Spiked, 20 April 2001.

81 Brendan O'Neill, 'At last, the myth of "institutional racism" is collapsing', Unherd, 31 March 2021.

82 Eric Kaufmann, 'Why the race equalities report is so subversive', Unherd, 31 March 2021.

83 Ayaan Hirsi Ali, 'Buffalo and the myth of racist America', Unherd, 18 May 2022.

84 Matthew Goodwin, 'Winning the culture wars', Substack, 26 July 2023.

85 Matthew Goodwin, 'What happened to me?', Substack, 23 October 2023.

86 Ford and Goodwin, op. cit.

87 Roger Eatwell and Matthew Goodwin, *National Populism: The Revolt against Liberal Democracy*, Pelican, p. 80.

88 Matthew Goodwin, 'The failures of British conservatism', National Conservative conference, 17 May 2023.

89 Matthew Goodwin, op. cit., *Sunday Times*, 2 June 2019.

90 Goodwin, 'Failures'.

91 Maurice Glasman, 'The future belongs to Blue Labour', Spiked, 5 November 2022.

92 Robert D. Kaplan, John Gray and Helen Thompson, 'The new age of tragedy', *New Statesman*, 26 April 2023.

93 David Goodhart, 'A postliberal future?, Demos, 2014.

94 Matthew Goodwin, *Values, Voice and Virtue*, Penguin, 2023, p. 33.

95 Ibid., p. 24.

96 Ibid., p. 32.

97 David Goodhart, *The Road to Somewhere*, Hurst, 2017, p. 2.

98 Ibid., p. 145.

99 Ibid., p. 4.

100 John Gray, 'Why liberals now believe in conspiracies', *New Statesman*, 14 August 2019.

101 John Gray, 'State of the nation', *New Statesman*, 8 July 2020.

102 John Gray, 'The woke have no vision of the future', Unherd, 17 June 2020.

103 Maurice Glasman, *New Statesman*, 17–23 January 2020.

104 Goodwin, *Values*, p. xi.

105 Ibid., p. 45.

106 John Gray, 'Woke'.

107 Ross Douthat, 'The rise of woke capital', *New York Times*, 28 February 2018.

108 Matthew Goodwin tweet, 6 December 2020.

109 Matt Goodwin, 'So why does nobody talk about these children?', *Daily Mail*, 3 April 2021.

110 Eatwell and Goodwin, op. cit., pp. 45–6.

111 David Goodhart, 'Too diverse?', *Prospect*, 20 February 2004.

112 David Goodhart, 'Progressive nationalism', Demos, May 2006.

113 David Goodhart, *The British Dream*, Atlantic, 2013, p. 13.

114 Goodhart, *Somewhere*, p. 32.

115 David Goodhart, 'How do we cut illegal immigration? By policing Britain's internal border', *Daily Telegraph*, 28 July 2018.

116 Rowena Davies, op. cit., pp. 194–6.

117 Ibid, pp. 209, 211.

118 Matthew Goodwin, 'Somebody needs to take control –

now', Substack, 2 July 2023.

119 Matthew Goodwin, 'What I told a cabinet minister', Substack, 31 August 2023.

120 Miriam Cates, 'Our declining birth rate', speech at National Conservative conference, 15 May 2023.

121 John Gray, 'The dangerous conceits of the green revolution', *New Statesman*, 16 November 2022.

122 Matthew Goodwin, 'The shifting politics of net zero', Substack, 8 August 2023.

123 'What is the Great Reset – and how did it get hijacked by conspiracy theories?', BBC Verify, 24 June 2021.

124 Goodhart, *Road to Somewhere*, p. 161.

125 David Goodhart, *Head Hand Heart*, Penguin, 2020, p. 147.

126 John Gray, 'Why Labour keeps losing', *New Statesman*, 15 January 2020.

127 Paul Embery, tweet, 7 April 2019.

128 Eric Kaufmann, *Whiteshift*, Allen Lane, 2018, pp. 1–2.

129 Flora Garamvolgyi and Peter Walker, 'Viktor Orban-influenced university plans outpost in London', *The Guardian*, 28 August 2023.

130 John Lloyd, 'Can Roger Scruton save the European Right?', Unherd, 14 April 2023.

131 Nick Cohen, 'Paranoid seductions: Sir Roger Scruton and the rise of the hard right', Substack, 26 July 2023.

132 ' The Roger Scruton interview: the full transcript', *New Statesman*, 26 April 2019.

133 Lloyd, op. cit.

134 Nick Timothy, 'There can never be One Nation if liberal Conservatives betray Brexit', *Daily Telegraph*, 29 May 2019.

135 John Gray, 'The fall of Liz Truss will not bring calm but rather a new period of conflict', *New Statesman*, 26 October 2022.

136 Suella Braverman, speech to Conservative Party Conference, 3 October 2023.

137 Matt Goodwin, 'Rise of the luxury belief class', Substack, 9 October 2023.

138 Matthew Goodwin, 'My night with Rishi', Substack, 13 February 2024.

139 Nesrine Malik, 'It's the culture war games – and the last Tory contenders are on the run from reality', *The Guardian*, 9 August 2022.

140 Davies and MacRae, op. cit., p. 21.

141 Heather Stewart and Aubrey Allegretti, 'Rishi Sunak seeks to revive faltering No 10 bid by attacking "woke nonsense"', *The Guardian*, 29 July 2022.

142 Ben Quinn and Angela Giuffrida, '"A love-burst": how Sunak and Meloni's rapport is boosting hard-right agenda', *The Guardian*, 16 December 2023.

143 Ibid.

144 John Lloyd, op. cit.

145 Matthew Goodwin, 'A reply to Dominic Cummings', Substack, 16 August 2023.

146 Matthew Goodwin, 'An open letter to Rishi Sunak', Substack, 29 January 2024.

147 Rishi Sunak, Speech text, Prime Minister's Office, 1 March 2024.

148 Matthew Goodwin, 'How Britain fights back', Substack, 4 March 2024.

149 Goodhart, *Somewhere*, p. 4.

150 Goodwin, *Values*, p. 11.

151 Summary report, 'Elitist Britain 2019: The educational background of Britain's leading people', The Sutton Trust and the Social Mobility Commission, 2019.

152 Goodwin, op. cit., p. xx.

153 Ibid., p. 30.

154 Ibid., p. 16.

155 Ibid., p. 18.

156 Ibid., p. 19.

157 Ibid., pp. 22–3.

158 Ibid., p. 18.

159 YouGov poll 2020, quoted by David Aaronovitch in a

debate with Matthew Goodwin, 'Is Britain run by an out of touch elite?', Prospect Podcasts, 25 October 2023.

160 Lord Ashcroft, 'How the United Kingdom voted on Thursday… and why', Lord Ashcroft polls, 24 June 2016.

161 'A liberalisation in attitudes?', National Centre for Social Research, 21 September 2023.

162 'UK public opinion toward immigration: overall attitudes and level of concern', summary of Ipsos Mori data, Migration Observatory, University of Oxford, 28 September 2023.

163 Patrick English, 'Is the stereotypical image of "Red Wall" residents actually accurate?", YouGov, 17 May 2021.

164 Quoted on *Dispatches*, Channel 4, 8 July 2019.

165 Kiran Stacey, 'Most party members say Islam is threat to British way of life – poll', *The Guardian*, 29 February 2024.

166 Victor E. Marsden (trans), *The Protocols of the Learned Elders of Zion*, Britons Publishing Company, 1968, p. 27.

167 Norman Cohn, *Warrant for Genocide*, Pelican, 1970.

168 Robert E. Welch, *The Blue Book of the John Birch Society*, American Opinion Books, 1961.

169 A.K. Chesterton, *The New Unhappy Lords*, Hampshire: Candour, 1965, p. 216.

170 Enoch Powell, speech at Chippenham, 11 May 1968.

171 Enoch Powell, speech at Wolverhampton, 11 June 1970.

172 Eatwell and Goodwin, *National Populism*, pp. 45–6.

173 Niraj Chokshi, 'Trump accuses Clinton of guiding global elite against US working class, *New York Times*, 13 October 2016.

174 Marsden, *Protocols*, p. 25.

175 Viktor Orban, Speech commemorating the 170th anniversary of the 1848 revolution, 15 March 2018, Freedom House, 4 April 2018.

176 The Covenant of the Hamas, https://irp.fas.org/world/para/docs/880818a.htm

177 Ilias Kasidiaris – see 'Golden Dawn (Greece)', Wikipedia.

178 Ascherson, op. cit.

179 Mikey Smith, 'Liz Truss blames "the Deep State" for "sabotaging" her 49 days as PM in Fox News tirade', *Daily Mirror*, 21 February 2024.

180 David Edgar, 'Gateway to the far right?', *Searchlight*, Summer 2003.

181 Danielle Kurtzleben, 'Why Trump's authoritarian language about "vermin" matters,, NPR, 17 November 2023.

182 Nathan Layne, 'Trump repeats "poisoning the blood" anti-immigrant remark', Reuters, 16 December 2023.

183 David Smith, '"It'll be bedlam": how Trump is creating conditions for a post-election eruption', *The Observer*, 23 March 2024.

184 Simon Cottee, 'The liberal fantasy of the Capitol coup', Unherd, 6 January 2022.

185 Martin Gurri, 'Why all this Trump hysteria?', Unherd, 6 December 2023.

186 Batya Ungar-Sargon, 'Is Trump on his way back to the White House?', Spiked, 7 November 2023.

187 Boris Johnson, 'The global wokerati are trembling so violently you can hear the ice tinkling in their negronis… but a Trump presidency could be just what the world needs', *Daily Mail*, 20 January 2024.

188 Eatwell and Goodwin, op. cit., p. 47.

189 Matthew Goodwin, tweet, 7 January 2021.

190 Matthew Goodwin, 'What New Hampshire is really all about', Substack, 22 January 2024.

191 For a catalogue of theories of fascism, see Paul Mason, *How to Stop Fascism*, Allen Lane, 2021, pp. 163–99.

192 Paxton, Robert, The Anatomy of Fascism, Alfred A. Knopf, 2004, p. 218.

193 Mason, op. cit., p. 165.

194 Paxton, Robert, 'The five stages of fascism', *Journal of Modern History*, March 1998, p. 24.

195 Fekete in Panitch and Albo, op. cit., p. 7.

196 David Smith, '"My ultimate and absolute revenge": Trump gives chilling CPAC speech on presidential election', *The*

Guardian, 25 February 2024.

197 Simon Heffer, 'Rise of the new working class Tories', *New Statesman*, 22 January 2020.

198 Szelenyi, op. cit. pp. 89, 120–1, 162, 286.

199 'What's happened to the 40 new hospitals pledge?', BBC Verify, 4 July 2022.

200 Martin Wolf, 'The levelling-up white paper is a necessary call to arms', *Financial Times*, 6 February 2022.

201 Jon Ungoed-Thomas, 'Affluent south-east gets more levelling up cash than north-east', *The Observer*, 4 September 2022.

202 *New Statesman* on Twitter, 5 August 2022.

203 Rajeev Syal, 'Rishi Sunak admits taking money from deprived areas', *The Guardian*, 5 August 2022.

204 Rachel Wolf, 'Johnson's re-set choice', Conservative Home, 14 November 2020.

205 Throughout the 2010s, with the exception of a short period in 2016, YouGov's tracker poll showed that the most important issue was either health or the economy. https://yougov.co.uk/topics/society/trackers/the-most-important-issues-facing-the-country

206 John Gray, 'The struggle for America's soul', *New Statesman*, 13 November 2020.

207 Suella Braverman, speech, Hansard, Volume 721, 31 October 2022.

208 Suella Braverman, speech, Hansard, Volume 729, 7 March 2023.

209 Jon Bloomfield, 'From Uganda to Rwanda: the British political class's ever-present hostility to 'aliens'', *Byline Times*, 23 May 2023.

210 Ibid.

211 Patrick Worrall, 'Boris Johnson falsely claims he didn't say anything about Turkey in the referendum campaign', Channel 4 Fact Check, 18 January 2019.

212 Alison Smale, 'Long dominated by the center, Austria splits to the left and right', *New York Times*, 16 May 2016.

213 Eatwell and Goodwin, op. cit., pp. 285–6.

214 'Danish prime minister wants country to accept "zero" asylum seekers', The Local Denmark, 22 January 2021.

215 Angelique Chrisafis, 'France passes controversial immigration bill amid deep division in Macron's party', *The Guardian*, 19 December 2023.

216 Unherd staff, 'Donald Tusk: mass migration is a "civilisational threat"', Unherd, 13 February 2024.

217 Joseph Rachman, 'Speaker at National Conservatism Conference accused of downplaying Holocaust after saying Germany "mucked up"', The Independent, 17 May 2023.

218 Andrew Witherspoon and Sam Levine, 'These maps show how Republicans are blatantly rigging elections', *The Guardian*, 12 November 2021.

219 Sam Levine, 'Trump suggests he will use FBI to go after political rivals if he returns to presidency', *The Guardian*, 11 November 2023.

220 'Open Society Barometer: Can Democracy Deliver?', Open Society Foundations, September 2023.

221 Tara John, 'More than half of UK voters want "strong, rule-breaking" leader, says survey', CNN, 8 April 2019.

222 Peter Thiel, 'The education of a libertarian', Cato Unbound, 13 April 2009.

223 Esther Addley, 'Study shows 60% of Britons believe in conspiracy theories', *The Guardian*, 23 November 2018.

224 Suella Braverman, 'Islamists are bullying Britain into submission', *Daily Telegraph*, 22 February 2024.

225 GB News, 23 February 2024.

226 See interview with Arnaud Montebourg, ex-socialist industry minister, *Le Monde*, 7 September 2019. Quoted in Jon Bloomfield, 'Limits of the nationalist left', Social Europe, 14 October 2019.

227 'Road goods vehicles travelling to Europe July 2022 to June 2023', Department for Transport, 10 August 2023.

228 Jonathan Rutherford, 'Labour must have the courage to reduce immigration', *New Statesman*, 7 December 2023.

229 'Europe's moment: Repair and Prepare for the Next Generation', COM/2020/456 final, Brussels, 27 May 2020.

230 Derek Brower, James Politi, Amanda Chu, 'The new era of big government: Biden rewrites the rules of economic policy', *Financial Times*, 13 July 2023.

231 Rachel Reeves, 'A new business model for Britain', Labour Together, 24 May 2023.

232 Pippa Crerar, 'Rachel Reeves rules out wealth tax if Labour wins next election', *The Guardian*, 27 August 2023.

233 Rachel Reeves, Mais Lecture 2024. UK Labour Press Release, 19 March 2024.

234 Thomas Piketty, *A Brief History of Equality*, Harvard University Press, 2022.

235 'Ending Stagnation: A New Economic Strategy for Britain, Resolution Foundation & Centre for Economic Performance', LSE, December 2023, p. 8.

236 Ibid.

237 For more see Andrew Marr, 'Even in a season of goodwill, I look back in anger at the Tory mess that was 2022', *New Statesman*, 7 December 2023; Martin Wolf, 'Britain desperately needs a growth strategy', *Financial Times*, 12 December 2023; Liam Byrne, *The Inequality of Wealth*, Apollo Books, 2024.

238 Flows Decree 2023–2025, https://www.altalex.com/documents/news/2023/07/12/decreto-flussi-2023-2025-ok-consiglio-ministri; Jacopo Barogazzi, 'How Italy's far-right leader learned to stop worrying and love migration', Politico, 30 August 2023.

239 Helena Smith, 'Greece to legalise papers for thousands of migrants to counter labour shortage', *The Guardian*, 19 December 2023.

240 Data drawn from ONS Census statistics 2021, 'Ethnic group, England and Wales', Office for National Statistics (ons.gov.uk).

241 A term first developed by Amartya Sen.

242 National Centre for Social Research, 2 November 2023. In 2002, assessing the impact of immigration on the country, just

17% said immigration had positive effects on the economy; by 2022 this had risen to 59%. On making the country a better place to live, the number observing positive effects rose from 20% to 56%.

243 Jon Bloomfield and David Edgar, 'Kicking back: why the Conservative 'culture wars' backfired',
Byline Times, 26 July 2021.

244 Tyrone Mings, tweet, 12 July 2021.

245 'Abortion rises in importance as a voting issue, driven by Democrats', Pew Research Centre, 23 August 2022.

246 https://www.iea.org/reports/renewables-2022/executive-summary

247 Lord (David) Frost, 'Rising temperatures likely to be beneficial for Britain', *Daily Telegraph*, 25 July 2023

248 John Gray, 'The dangerous conceits of the green revolution', *New Statesman*, 16 November 2023.

249 EV-Volumes: The Electric Vehicle World Sales Database – see EV Volumes.com

250 Keir Starmer and Rachel Reeves:, 'Circumstances have changed, our ambitions have not', *The Guardian*, 8 February 2024.

251 Federal Subsidy for Efficient Buildings (BEG) by KfW, IEA, 3 May 2022.

252 'MaPrimeRénov' evolves: new products in 2023', https://www.service-public.fr/particuliers/actualites/A16350?lang=en

253 Editorial on technical education: 'Manchester can blaze a trail', *The Guardian*, 17 May 2023.

254 Matthew Goodwin, 'Why those blaming Brexit for Britain's ills are completely WRONG', *Daily Express*, 22 May 2023.

255 Statista Research Department, 16 January 2024. As of December 2023, 55% of people in Great Britain thought that it was wrong to leave the European Union, compared with 33% who thought it was the right decision.

256 Peter Kellner, 'What should Labour's Brexit policy be? An immediate return to the EU is out of the question. But restoring frictionless trade is vital', *Prospect*, 22 November 2022.

QUESTIONS TO CONSIDER

1. How important has the decline of social-democratic parties across Europe been for the rise of national populism?

2. What were the causes of the rise of national populism in Europe, America and beyond, in the 2010s and 2020s?

3. What are the issues that have had the most appeal to national populist voters?

4. Pre-war, the far right claimed that black people and Jews were inferior. Today, following the writings of the French philosopher Alain de Benoist, they prefer to talk about the intrinsic differences between cultures. How should progressives counter this shift in argument?

5. Has national populism redrawn the ideological faultline of politics, and, if so, in what way?

6. Mussolini used the slogan 'Diu, patria e famiglia'. Italian Prime Minister Giorgia Meloni repeats it today. The Nazis used the slogan 'Kinder, Kuche, Kirche'. Blue Labour was launched under the slogan 'Faith, flag and family', used now by the New Conservatives

group and Matthew Goodwin. What are the problems with this slogan?

7. National populist pundits and politicians have invented a new language which sneers at progressives – new elite, the blob, luxury beliefs, woke etc. This populist lexicon is increasingly used in the press and media. What could be your riposte if someone uses these terms in an argument or discussion?

8. How can progressive forces counter the populist right; halt its advance and offer a positive vision for the future?